GENETIC FINGERPRINTING
THE LAW AND SCIENCE OF DNA

GENETIC FINGERPRINTING
THE LAW AND SCIENCE OF DNA

Judge Gerald Sheindlin

Rutledge Books, Inc.

Bethel, CT

Rutledge Books, Inc.
Bethel, CT 06801

Printed in the United States of America

Library of Congress Cataloging-in-Publication Data
Sheindlin, Gerald
    Genetic fingerprinting : the law and science
of DNA / Gerald Sheindlin
        p. cm.
    ISBN 1-88750-04-5
    ① DNA fingerprinting- -United States. ② Evidence,
Expert- -United States. ③ Forensic genetics- -United States.
① Title.
KF9667.S54 1996   95-71352
614.1- -dc20   CIP

ACKNOWLEDGEMENTS

The sweeping scope of this book would be impossible to compile without the aid and advice of numerous legal and scientific experts. I wish to acknowledge the following people who have deeply influenced me. They have created the setting to inspire me to become involved in the intriguing topic of DNA forensic evidence and they have significantly contributed, directly and indirectly, to the writing of this book:

Peter Coddington, the chief of the appeals bureau of the District Attorney's Office in Bronx County; Risa Sugarman, a senior trial prosecutor in Bronx County who, along with Peter Coddington, was one of the prosecutors in the Castro case; Peter Neufeld and Prof. Barry Scheck, the defense attorneys in the Castro case and members of the defense team in the infamous O.J. Simpson murder case; George "Woody" Clark and Rockne "Rock" Harmon, prosecutors from California and members of the prosecution team in the O.J. Simpson murder case; Dr. Eric Lander, an expert witness in the Castro case and who has been described by some as one of the five smartest people in the world; Dr. Bruce Budowle, the chief scientist for the FBI; Dr. Lorraine Flaherty, a geneticist and expert witness in the Castro case; Dr. Henry Lee, a renowned forensic scientist and an expert witness in the Simpson murder case; Justice Burton B. Roberts, my boss; Julia Davis, my court attorney; Moshe Siegel, my former court attorney; Judge Herbert J. Adlerberg, my former law partner for 20 years; Irving Mendelson, my mentor and guide for 14 years; finally, my wife, Judge Judith Sheindlin (although she prefers if I call her "Your Honor") and my children, Greg, Jamie, Jon, Adam and Nicole. I can't seem to do anything without them.

TABLE OF CONTENTS

SECTION A

TABLE OF CASES (ALPHABETICAL)

Genetic Fingerprinting:

Genetic Fingerprinting:

Genetic Fingerprinting:

TABLE OF CASES (BY STATE)

CALIFORNIA

COLORADO

KENTUCKY

LOUISIANA

MARYLAND

MASSACHUSETTS

MICHIGAN

MINNESOTA

MISSISSIPPI

MISSOURI

MONTANA

NEBRASKA

NEW HAMPSHIRE

NEW JERSEY

NEW MEXICO

NEW YORK

Genetic Fingerprinting:

NORTH CAROLINA

OHIO

OKLAHOMA

OREGON

PENNSYLVANIA

SOUTH CAROLINA

SOUTH DAKOTA

Genetic Fingerprinting:

VIRGINIA

WASHINGTON

WEST VIRGINIA

WYOMING

FEDERAL JURISDICTION

SECTION B

TABLE OF STATUTES

STATE	SECTION

Genetic Fingerprinting:

SECTION C

TABLE OF AUTHORITIES

*Validation Studies on the Analysis of the HLA DQ Alpha Locus
Using the Polymerase Chain Reaction*
  36 Journal of Forensic Sciences, Pg. 1644, 1647
  (Nov. 1994) . . . . G§5 (b)

VNTR Population Data: A Worldwide Study
  Federal Bureau of Investigation, 1993 . . . . G-7 (b)

*The Assessment of Frequency Estimates of Hae 111-Generated VNTR
Profiles in Various Reference Databases,*
  39 Journal of Forensic Sciences Pg. 319-352,
  (March, 1994) . . . . .G-7 (b)

*Evaluation of Hinf 1-Generated VNTR Profiles Using Various Ethnic
Databases,*
  39 Journal of Forensic Sciences Pg. 988-1008,
  (July, 1994) . . . . .G-7 (b)

*The Polymerase Chain Reaction (PCR): The Second Generation of DNA
Analysis Methods Takes The Stand*
  9 Computer and High Technology Law Journal 314
  (1993) . . . . .G-5 (b)

SECTION D

INTRODUCTION

Many young men attack a jogger in Central park. Several point to the other as the rapist. Sperm is obtained from the victim.

A drifter gets into Bellevue hospital and murders a young doctor. When arrested, he has blood on his clothes which are seized.

A 57 year old lady with Alzheimer's disease is raped. She is incapable of identifying her assailant. Only a bus driver who drove her to a day care center that day had access to her. Sperm was removed from the victim and tested against the defendant's blood.

A Palo Verde seed is found in the rear of the defendant's truck. DNA from the seed is compared with the DNA of a Palo Verde tree under which the deceased's body was found.

Each of these examples and many hundreds...and perhaps thousands more in the United States, offer the judicial system an opportunity to use a powerful new technology for identifying criminal suspects—the technology of DNA fingerprinting or typing.

No other blood test or serum test rivals the power and accuracy of DNA. Under ideal conditions and testing circumstances, the probability of two individuals sharing the same DNA pattern by chance is about one in 30 billion. There are only 6 billion people on earth. With odds so infinitesimally small, DNA rivals the power of fingerprint evidence.

DNA tests have 5 major forensic applications:

1. DNA can identify and link suspects to a crime. Suspects can be identified and linked in criminal cases, such as rape cases. Fingerprints link a person circumstantially to the crime scene or weapon, but DNA often links the suspect to the crime itself.

2. DNA can distinguish between types of crimes. "Serial" crimes can be differentiated from "copy-cat" crimes. By comparing the DNA from multiple crime scenes, police can determine if more than one perpetrator was involved or if the same person committed the crimes.

3. DNA can exculpate wrongly accused persons. In *People v. Lindsey Calhoun*, a rape case recently decided by me, DNA tests showed conclusively that the DNA recovered from the sperm did not match the defendant's DNA profile. I dismissed the indictment. In fact, as a judge, I have had more dismissals based on DNA forensic evidence than convictions.

4. DNA can be used to identify the remains of a victim. Tissue found on the grill of a car was determined to be a specific victim, by comparing the DNA from the tissue with that of the victims parents. Also, remains of a soldier can lead to the soldiers identity. By the year 1999, the Department of Defense plans to obtain and store blood samples from every member of the armed forces. In addition, by the year 2005, every member of the armed forces reserves will donate blood samples. The purpose of this procedure is to act as "genetic dogtags", permitting identification in the event of a tragedy.

5. DNA can determine the paternity in civil cases. In Paternity cases, DNA can tell if two people are related by comparing their DNA, as the child gets half the DNA from the father and half from the mother. One such example would be the screening of immigrants who claim a blood relation with U.S. citizens.

Accordingly, it is obvious that the power of the tests is enormous, if properly conducted.

DNA tests were initially developed in a diagnostic setting to aid in the identification of genes in a chromosome which caused inherited diseases.

DNA diagnostic tests have advanced so that presently, DNA evaluation has helped identify defective DNA associated with Huntington's disease, Duchenne muscular dystrophy, sickle cell disease, cystic fibrosis and retinoblastoma. In retinoblastoma, a cancer of the eye which afflicts 1 in every 15,000 children born in the United States, DNA testing has proven invaluable in early diagnosis and successful treatment of this form of cancer.

However, the use of these tests in a forensic setting is of very recent origin.

Bodily fluids, when present at the scene of a crime, can produce valuable DNA identification evidence, capable of swiftly convicting the guilty and exonerating the innocent. Clearly, it is valuable scientific evidence in criminal cases.

Most courts in the United States, including the U.S. District Courts and the Federal Circuit Courts of Appeals, have ruled that DNA identification evidence is admissible in criminal trials. Some states have used the *Frye* standard [*Frye v. United States*, 293 F.1013 (D.C. Cir 1923)] which is the prevailing rule in New York State. *People v. Wesley*, 83 N.Y.2d. 417 (1994); *People v. Middleton*, 54 N.Y.2d 42 (1981). Other jurisdictions have reached the same result under Federal Rules of Evidence 403 and 702 or a similar standard of "relevancy."

Genetic Fingerprinting:

Some states have enacted legislation that create investigative DNA data-banks designed to collect DNA evidence for use in future investigations and criminal trials. For example, the New York Legislature recently enacted legislation establishing a DNA databank. Some states have mandated the admission of DNA evidence through legislation.

This book will analyze the science underlying the use of DNA forensic evidence and the major federal and state cases which have decided issues relating to this evidence.

First, an "Overview of the Law in the United States" will set forth a brief analysis of the number of states deciding specific DNA issues.

Second, a "Brief Guide by Jurisdiction" will be presented as an aid to quickly identify a specific issue by state or federal jurisdiction.

Next, "Understanding the Basic Science" will set forth the fundamental science justifying the use of DNA forensic evidence. The strengths, the weaknesses, and the controversy surrounding its use will be discussed. Annexed to this chapter is a summary of the 1992 report issued by the National Research Council entitled "DNA Technology in Forensic Science."

Included is an outline "A Comparison Between PCR and RFLP", comparing and indicating various distinctions between the DNA tests.

Thereafter, in "DNA Cases by Jurisdiction", legal holdings of the individual cases will be discussed in alphabetical order of the states jurisdiction followed by the federal jurisdiction. Where fact patterns are unusual or the investigation particularly interesting, factual details and the DNA forensic test results will be set forth, along with the court's legal holding.

Finally, a "Glossary of Terms Commonly Used In DNA Forensic Analysis" is annexed.

OVERVIEW OF THE LAW IN THE UNITED STATES

No jurisdiction has ruled that DNA identification evidence is *per se* inadmissible. Thirty jurisdictions[1] and the United States Court of Appeals for the Second and Eighth Circuits have declared that DNA evidence is admissible both to include and exclude identity. Ten jurisdictions[2] and the Second and Eighth Circuits have held that no pretrial hearing is required before the evidence is admitted. Sixteen jurisdictions[3] have ruled that defects in the performance of the DNA testing procedures go to the weight of the evidence and not its admissibility. Seven jurisdictions[4] have ruled that DNA identification is reliable and should be admitted if the tests are performed properly, but will exclude the evidence if significant laboratory error is established. Seven jurisdictions[5] have decided that DNA evidence should be admitted but have placed limitations on statistical evidence. The law of California may now be settled.[6]

BRIEF GUIDE BY JURISDICTION

Key Words:
1) Whether DNA admitted or not admitted
2) Name of laboratory performing test
3) Test performed— RFLP or PCR or both
4) Standard of admissibility—Frye, relevancy statute or case law or combination
5) Whether statistics admitted
6) Method used to calculate statistics—product rule, ceiling principle (per NRC), fixed or floating bins
7) Miscellaneous comments
8) Year of latest decision

Order of key word sequence is as follows:
1) Admitted or not admitted
2) Lab
3) Test performed
4) Standard of Admissibility
5) Statistics admitted
6) Method of calculation
7) Miscellaneous comments
8) Year of latest decision

ALABAMA:

Admitted/Lifecodes: RFLP/*Frye*/statistics admitted: ceiling method and product rule admissible (foundational hearing required per *Castro*) (1995)

ARIZONA:

Admitted/Cellmark: RFLP/*Frye* satisfied/statistics not admissible: product rule fails *Frye* (1995)

ARKANSAS:

Admitted/FBI: RFLP/state statute/statistics admitted: fixed bin (no defense) (1994)

* **CALIFORNIA**: ("*" = State has diverse holdings.)

California v. Amundson: Admitted/Cellmark: RFLP/PCR/ statistics admitted: Ceiling principle (1995)

California v. Axell: Admitted/Cellmark: RFLP/*Kelly-Frye*/ statistics admitted: product rule (1991)

California v. Barney: Not admitted/Cellmark and FBI: RFLP/product rule not admissible/test foundation inadequate (1992)

California v. Burks: Admitted/Cellmark: RFLP/statistics admitted: Ceiling principle (1995)

California v. Marlow: Admitted/Cellmark: RFLP/statistics admitted: product rule; foundation acceptable; rejects *Barney* & accepts *Axell* principles (1995)

California v. McSherry: Admitted/Forensic Science: PCR DQ-Alpha; Defendant excluded; possible contamination and new trial denied (1992)

California v. Pizzaro: Not admitted/FBI: RFLP/product rule not admitted; foundation inadequate (1992)

California v. Soto: Admitted/County Lab: RFLP/statistics admitted: product rule, fixed bin and floating bin; foundation acceptable; rejects *Barney* & accepts *Axell* principles (1994)

California v. Wilds: Admitted/Cellmark: RFLP/statistics admitted: product rule; foundation acceptable; rejects *Barney* & accepts*Axell* principles (1995)

COLORADO:

Admitted/Cellmark: RFLP/*Frye*/statistics admitted: product rule (1993)

CONNECTICUT:

Admitted/Cellmark: RFLP/remanded for ceiling principle per NRC (1995)

DELAWARE:

Not admitted/Cellmark: RFLP/*Frye* and state statute/product rule prejudicial (1993)

DISTRICT OF COLUMBIA:

Admitted/FBI: RFLP/state statute/statistics admitted: ceiling principle (1994)

FLORIDA:

Admitted/Lifecodes and FBI: RFLP/relevancy/statistics admitted: "binning" method, ceiling principle to be considered; "band shifting" fails *Frye* (1995)

GEORGIA:

Admitted/Lifecodes: RFLP/state case law/statistics not admitted on facts of case (1994); PCR admitted(1995)

HAWAII:

Admitted/FBI: RFLP/*Frye* and state statute/statistics admitted: "binning" method (1992)

ILLINOIS:

Admitted/Lifecodes, Cellmark and FBI: RFLP/statistics admitted: product rule and "binning" method (1994)

INDIANA:

Admitted/Cellmark: RFLP/*Frye*/test goes to weight (1993)

IOWA:

> Admitted/RFLP/state statute/statistics admitted: product rule (test goes to weight) (1994)

** **KANSAS**: *("**"* = Experts allowed to give diverse opinions.)

> Admitted/Lifecodes: RFLP/*Frye*/statistics admitted: product rule (1993)

** **KENTUCKY**:

> Admitted/FBI: RFLP/*Frye*/statistics admitted: "binning" method (1992)

LOUISIANA:

> Admitted/Cellmark: RFLP/state statute and caselaw/ statistics admitted: product rule (1994)

MARYLAND:

> Admitted/Cellmark: RFLP/*Frye*/*Reed* and state statute (no defense) (1992)

* **MASSACHUSETTS**:

> *Massachusetts v. Curnin*: Admitted with modifications/ Cellmark: RFLP/*Frye*/statistics not admitted (1991)

** *Massachusetts v. Daggett*: Admitted/Cellmark: RFLP/*Frye*/ statistics not admitted (1993)

> *Massachusetts v. Lanigan*: Admitted/FBI: RFLP/*Frye*/ statistics admitted:ceiling principle (1994)

** *Massachusetts v. Vega*: Admitted/Lifecodes: RFLP/*Frye*/ statistics admitted: product rule (1994)

MICHIGAN:

Admitted/Cellmark: RFLP/*Davis-Frye*/statistics admitted: (need foundational hearing) (1994)

MINNESOTA:

Admitted/FBI: RFLP/*Frye*, relevance and state statute/ "band shift" goes to weight/statistics admitted: ceiling principle/PCR affirmed (1994)

MISSISSIPPI:

RFLP acceptable (1993)

MISSOURI:

Admitted/Cellmark: RFLP/*Frye*/statistics admitted: (1995)

** **MONTANA:**

Admitted/Cellmark: RFLP and PCR/no statistics offered per defense request. (1995)

** **NEBRASKA:**

Not admitted/Lifecodes: RFLP (meets *Frye*)/statistics not admitted: product rule fails *Frye*/PCR admissible/ statistics for both tests admissible if NRC ceiling method used (1994)

NEW HAMPSHIRE:

Admitted/FBI: RFLP/*Frye*/statistics admitted: "binning" method and ceiling principle accepted (no foundational hearing) (1995)

NEW JERSEY:

Admitted/Cetus: PCR and GM/KM/modified *Frye*/ statistics admitted: product rule (1994)

NEW MEXICO:

> Admitted/FBI: RFLP/*Frye* and state case law/statistics admitted: "binning" method (1994)

NEW YORK:

> Admitted/Lifecodes: RFLP/*Frye*/statistics admitted: product rule (need foundational hearing) (1995)

** **NORTH CAROLINA**:

> Admitted/Cellmark and FBI: RFLP/state case law—not *Frye*/statistics admitted: "binning" method (no defense) (1995)

OHIO:

> Admitted/Cellmark/relevancy and state statute/statistics admitted: product rule (no foundational hearing) (1995)

OKLAHOMA:

> Admitted/RFLP/*Daubert*/statistics admitted: "binning." (1995)

OREGON:

> Admitted/Lifecodes: RFLP/state case law and statute/ statistics admitted: "band shift," ceiling and product rule (1993)

** **PENNSYLVANIA**:

> Admitted/Lifecodes: RFLP/*Frye*/statistics not admitted (no foundational hearing) (1994)

SOUTH CAROLINA:

> Admitted/Lifecodes: RFLP/*Frye* (no foundational hearing) statistics admitted: product rule (1995)

Genetic Fingerprinting:

SOUTH DAKOTA:

> Admitted/FBI: RFLP/*Frye* (foundational hearing required) (1991)

** **TENNESSEE:**

> Admitted/FBI: RFLP/state statute/statistics admitted: "binning" method (1994)

** **TEXAS:**

> Admitted/FBI: RFLP and PCR/state statute and case law/ statistics admitted: "binning" method (1994)

VERMONT:

> Admitted/FBI: RFLP/*Daubert;* statistics admitted: ceiling principle only. (1995)

VIRGINIA:

> Admitted/Lifecodes and FBI: RFLP/*Frye* and state case law/statistics admitted: "binning" method and product rule (1994)

** **WASHINGTON:**

> Admitted/Forensic Science: PCR/Lifecodes: RFLP/*Frye*/ statistics admitted: product rule (1995)

WEST VIRGINIA:

> Admitted/Cellmark: RFLP/*Frye* and state statute (test goes to weight) (1989)

WYOMING:

> Admitted/FBI: RFLP/state statute and case law/statistics admitted: "binning" method (1993)

UNITED STATES COURTS

COURT OF APPEALS:

Second Circuit:
U.S. v. Jakobetz:
> Admitted/FBI: RFLP/*Frye* and Fed. Rules Evid.
> (no foundational hearing required) (1992)

Fourth Circuit:
Spencer v. Murray:
> Admitted/FBI: RFLP/Fed. Rules Evid./statistics
> admitted: "binning" method (1993)

Sixth Circuit:
U.S. v. Yee:
> Admitted/FBI: RFLP/*Frye*/statistics admitted:
> "binning" method (1993)

Eighth Circuit:
U.S. v. Johnson:
> Admitted/FBI: RFLP/*Daubert*/statistics admitted:
> Ceiling principle (1995)

U.S. v. Martinez:
> Admitted/FBI: RFLP/*Daubert*/statistics admitted
> (1993)

U.S. v. Two Bulls:
> Admitted/FBI: RFLP/remanded for *Castro*
> hearing (1990)

Tenth Circuit:
U.S. v. Davis and Reed:
> Admitted/FBI: RFLP/*Daubert* and *Frye*/statistics
> admitted: "binning" method (1994)

DISTRICT COURTS:

Northern District of South Dakota:
U.S. v. Young:
  Admitted/Cellmark: RFLP/Fed. Rules Evid./
  statistics admitted (no objection) (1990)

SECTION G

DNA FORENSIC EVIDENCE: UNDERSTANDING THE BASIC SCIENCE

1 Introduction:

This review, analyzing the scientific basis for the use of DNA testing as evidence of identification in criminal cases, has been written by a judge, a non-scientist. It is intended to give the bare essentials of the science, and is a skeleton of the science designed for anyone who wants to understand a DNA case. The discussion provides the basic scientific justification for the use of DNA as evidence in identification. It will provide a description of how this evidence is created in the laboratory and how the technology can err. It will set forth the controls that should be in place to minimize the possibility of laboratory error. The basic principles of population genetics will be explained. Further, an analysis of how it is used to calculate the likelihood that a match between a suspect and forensic sample could be duplicated will be discussed. A basic analysis will set forth the current scientific controversies regarding these subjects which have affected the admissibility of this evidence.

After you have read this review, you should feel prepared to discuss the scientific aspects of DNA. The lawyer should have some understanding of the contents of an expert's testimony, whether it be on direct or cross examination. The lawyer should also gain some better understanding of what the direct or cross examination is trying to prove. An understanding of this section should aid a judge in formulating rulings before and during the hearing or trial. It will aid the judge, lawyer and lay person in understanding the rulings of the various courts in this area. Finally, everyone should be able to describe DNA forensic evidence in terms that the average person will understand. That is my objective.

This material may seem extremely complicated and difficult at first, but the complication chiefly stems from terminology. Once you understand what the words mean,[7] the concepts themselves (apart from the mathematics) are not complex. If you can remember, *At The Grand Concourse*, i.e., **A** Binds with **T** and **G** binds with **C**, and that it cannot happen any other way, you are on your way to understanding a DNA case.

2 Overview Of Human Genetics:

DNA, deoxyribonucleic acid, is the master genetic control, the fundamental material which determines the genetic characteristics, growth and development of all life forms. Humans have human forms and elephants have elephant form because of differences in the makeup of their respective

DNA. DNA's fundamental physical structure is the same regardless of the type of genetic creature it creates. DNA is composed of a long double helix, which looks like a spiral staircase. The backbone of this molecule (i.e., the handrails and balustrade of the staircase) consists of repeated sequences of phosphate and deoxyribose sugar. Attached to the sugar links in the backbone are two kinds of purines: Adenine (A) and Guanine (G); and two pyrimidines: Cytosine (C) and Thymine (T).[8] The purines and pyrimidines each combine to form a nucleotide (i.e., the steps of the staircase) which are held together by hydrogen bonds—two bonds in the case of A and T, and three bonds in the case of G and C *(see Figure I)*.

Because the chemical nature of the bond or attachment differs, only A and T can bond together, and only C and G can bond together. A cannot bond with G, and C cannot bond with T. Thus, the only possible combinations which can form the steps of the staircase are A-T, T-A, C-G, and G-C. That is the alphabet of the language of DNA. It consists of just four letters. Just as the order of the twenty-six letters in our alphabet form the words that we use, so too does the order of the four letters of the DNA alphabet define the living form.

Every cell that contains a nucleus contains DNA. There are approximately 100 trillion cells in the human body, and most contain DNA. Each human cell with a nucleus contains all the information necessary to produce a human body. This human blueprint is carried in packages of information known as chromosomes. The material of which they are made is called DNA. Red blood cells which do not have nuclei are a significant exception. A single DNA molecule consists of about three billion base pairs, all very tightly wound around each other in a winding fashion. Although this molecule is much too small to be seen by even the most powerful microscope, if it were stretched out to its full length, it would be about six feet long, and— if reduced to a written representation it would resemble: "CCGGTAGAT-ACCTG....etc."

The genetic information contained in a single human DNA molecule located in the nucleus of a single cell would fill about one hundred and twenty-five Manhattan telephone books. Within humans, as a species, much of the DNA molecule is identical. It is this identity of DNA that makes all humans look like humans, rather than, say, elephants or rubber trees.[9] We humans create human offspring by transferring our DNA to our children. The science of genetics studies how and why this happens.

Each normal human has forty-six chromosomes *[see Figure I(a)]*. Each chromosome is made up of DNA. Twenty-two of these chromosomes come from the mother and twenty-two come from the father. These are arranged in pairs and are numbered sequentially according to size. During reproduction

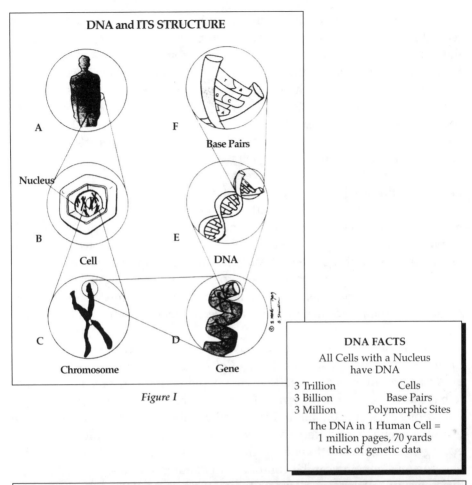

DNA and ITS STRUCTURE

A

Nucleus

B

C

Cell

Chromosome

F

Base Pairs

E

DNA

D

Gene

Figure I

DNA FACTS

All Cells with a Nucleus
have DNA

3 Trillion	Cells
3 Billion	Base Pairs
3 Million	Polymorphic Sites

The DNA in 1 Human Cell =
1 million pages, 70 yards
thick of genetic data

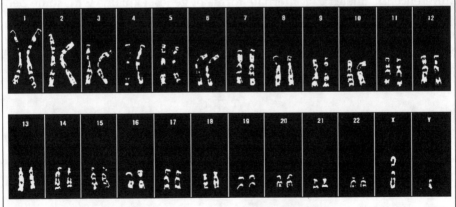

Figure I(a) - All 46 Chromosomes (23 pairs) of human male appear in this chart; a female would differ only in having two X chromosomes instead of X and Y (opposite).

the chromosome pairs of the mother and the father all split apart and then recombine—one chromosome from the mother and one chromosome from the father—to create the "new" twenty-two chromosome pairs of their child. Each individual's DNA is, therefore, unique, except for identical twins. At fertilization, the sperm which contains 23 chromosomes, combines with the ovum, which also contains 23 chromosomes, producing a total of 46 chromosomes in each cell. Two sex-typing chromosomes, denominated "X" and "Y" are also present. Females have two "X" chromosomes and males have one "X" and one "Y" chromosome, which make up a part of the total of forty-six chromosomes.[10] Therefore, fifty percent of the genetic information is of maternal origin and fifty percent is of paternal origin.

Each of us have about one hundred thousand genes. Hence, there are many, many genes on each chromosome. A gene is a stretch of DNA that is responsible for making a protein or other chemical necessary for the manufacture of a living thing. All of these genes and all of these chromosomes are composed primarily of DNA. This total pool of genetic information is known as the human genome. Under the correct circumstances, DNA is remarkably stable. For example, it has been extracted from Egyptian mummies.

Within each human there are obvious genetic differences, or alternate forms of genes, which are known as *alleles*. For example, the gene for blue eyes and brown eyes are well known; people with green eyes may be said to have an "allele" or an alternate form of the blue-eyed gene, while people with violet eyes may be said to have another "allele" or alternate form of the blue-eyed gene. This difference in eye color between two people with "blue-eyed genes," or this difference in their "alleles", forms the basis by which one person's genome can be compared to another's. In the medical field, a difference in "alleles", or alternate forms of genes, explains why some people contract Huntington's disease and some do not.

In chemical terms, the difference in alleles is explained by the difference in the ways the nucleotides (base pairs) arrange themselves along the DNA molecule. For example, one very short strand of DNA might look like

A T T C

T A A G

while another might look like

A T A C

T A T G

Genetic Fingerprinting:

and a third might look like

C A A T

G T T A

All are slightly different. Each is an allele. Each is an alternate form of the same gene. In actuality, however, each allele is much longer, i.e., on the order of 1,000 to 10,000 base pairs, or kilobases (KB), long. Each base pair consists of a single nucleotide, that one bond between A and T or C and G.[11] Very small variations in the order in which these base pairs occur on the DNA molecule can make huge differences. For example, Sickle-cell anemia is caused by a single base pair on chromosome 11 occurring out of order. If that single aberrant base pair were placed properly, that sufferer would have no disease. Lou Gehrig's disease occurs because of a misplaced base pair on chromosome 21.

Of the three billion base pairs in the human genome, scientists have been able to discover the known function of some of the genes. They produce arms, or legs, or kidneys, or toe nails, or brain cells. In each individual, the DNA which forms the genetic material needed to create these parts of our bodies are virtually identical with that of another person. Again, one human's leg resembles another human's leg more than it resembles an elephant's leg. This portion of the human genome has been mapped by the human gene mapping conference. But a portion of the human genome has no current known function, i.e., it does not appear to code for proteins. Hence, they do not appear to be genes. Science has not yet discovered what function, if any, it performs. If you could compare the genes with the pages of an instruction manual, between the pages that show how to construct the object, there are pages which contain no known language. We cannot seem to decipher this language, but we suspect it may be of some, or perhaps great, significance. Within this unknown, or non-coding, or polymorphic, region of the genome, some of which appears on each of the forty six chromosomes, there can be great differences between individuals in the way base pairs are arranged.[12] The difference in the length of the repeating base pairs in the region between the genes is the foundation upon which DNA identification rests. This repetition of base pairs occurs again and again. It can be compared to a page of a telephone book which repeats the surnames on one page again and again. It may appear to be a manufacturing error, but in the chromosomes no one yet has discovered the reason for this repetition. The important point that must be noted is that these variable repeating base pairs between genes do exist and vary greatly among individuals. This is known as a "Variable Number of Tandem Repeats" or "VNTR". This difference in repetition can also be compared to telephone books containing the name *Roberts*. In Manhattan, there may exist a much greater number of these names than in the telephone directory of Mariscopa County, Arizona. DNA is unique in this area, but only a small portion of the DNA segment is examined. Nonetheless, if you examine enough small sections of DNA in different chromosomes, scientists have established that you can reliably distinguish one person from another. This is the basis of DNA forensic evidence.

3 Southern Blotting and RFLP Identification:

There are two methods by which these differences in the DNA portions of the genome can be revealed and measured, to wit: "RFLP" and "PCR".

The first scientific process, RFLP, is accomplished by "Southern Blotting,"and is named for Dr. Edward Southern who invented the procedure in 1975. There are eight steps to this process [*see Figure 1(b) and 1(c)*]:

(1) extraction of the DNA from the forensic specimen
(2) digestion of DNA into fragments by restriction enzymes
(3) separation of the DNA fragments by electrophoresis
(4) staining the separated fragments with ethidium bromide so that they can be illuminated by ultraviolet exposure
(5) denaturing, or separating, the two DNA strands and fixing them to a nylon membrane
(6) hybridization of the single strand of DNA by marking it at a specific location with a radioactive probe
(7) reproducing a picture of the radioactively marked DNA onto an x-ray film—or autoradiograph
(8) calculating the probabilities of a match.

The following is a brief discussion of each step:

3(a)   Extraction of the DNA:

The extraction of DNA from the cells under examination begins with lysis, i.e., puncturing the cell with a mild detergent (typically Sodium Dodecyl Sulfate, or SDS), which allows the cellular material to escape. Then the proteins are broken down with an enzyme (usually Proteinase K) thus separating the DNA from the non-DNA material present in the solution. The non-DNA material is then extracted and the DNA is concentrated by precipitation with alcohol or by ultrafiltration with membranes that retain the DNA molecules due to their large molecular mass.

Genetic Fingerprinting:

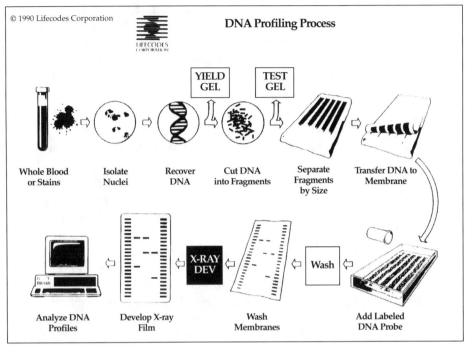

Figure 1(b)

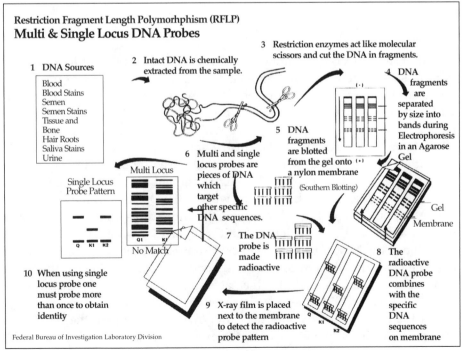

Figure 1(c)

Additional steps are needed in rape cases when the DNA is found on a swab taken from the victim's vagina because the swab typically contains semen from the rapist and epithelial cells[13] from the victim, both of which contain DNA. In 1986, scientists discovered that spermatozoa was more resistant to lysis than other cells, and that if the mixture containing both types of cells was exposed to a mild detergent, the sperm heads remained intact after the other cells had broken down. Thus, it was important to separate the sperm heads which was accomplished by low speed centrifugation (5000 to 15,000 X g). Once the sperm heads had been separated, then they could be punctured (lysed) by adding the reducing agent dithiothreitol to the detergent mixture which caused the thiol proteins to break up the sperm head, spilling out the inner DNA. Thus, as long as the forensic sample contains intact sperm heads, the DNA can be separated into the rapist's contribution and the victim's contribution.

In 1991, in addition to the usual lysis and the lysis performed in rape cases, a third preliminary technique was developed to recover DNA for PCR[14] analysis from extremely small forensic samples. This was accomplished by absorbing the DNA from the sample onto an ion exchange resin called Chelex and then removing the resin by boiling. As a result, DNA can be recovered from the epithelial cells found on cigarette butts, envelopes, or postage stamps.

3(b) Digestion:

After the DNA is extracted from the nucleus of the cells under examination, it is separated—or digested—into fragments for further examination by the application of a restriction enzyme. A restriction enzyme is a protein which chemically cuts a DNA molecule at a specific site which only it and its isoschizomers (i.e., other enzymes that cut the DNA in the same place) recognize.   For example, the restriction enzyme known as PST 1 (Providentia Stuartii #1), which was initially used by Lifecodes Corp., recognized the base pair sequence CTGCAG and cut the DNA between the A and G nucleotide. Thus, this enzyme will cut the DNA molecule at this specific A-G point at all places throughout the entire three billion base pairs in which the six base pair sequence that it recognizes occurs. The FBI and the DNA lab at the New York City Medical Examiner's office use the restriction enzyme HAE III, which recognizes the sequence GGCC and cuts the DNA between the G and the C. HAE III creates somewhat shorter fragments than does PST 1. As of 1994, Lifecodes has switched to HAE III.

In the area of the genome that is known and mapped, the restriction enzyme will cut everyone's DNA in the exact same places, resulting in DNA fragments which are of similar length. However, in the anonymous sequence where there are vast differences in the way the nucleotides are arranged, there will be great differences in the length of the fragment because of the varying number of nucleotides that lie between the cutting points that the restriction enzyme selects. These varying number of nucleotides are known by scientists as "Variable Number of Tandem Repeats" or repeat sequences of DNA base pairs which vary in length. They are called "VNTR" for short. The varying lengths of fragments produced by VNTR's after the DNA is cut by the restriction enzyme are known as "Restriction Fragment Length Polymorphisms," or RFLPs. In layman's terms, this means that RFLPs are fragments which have a different length because each RFLP has a variable number of VNTRs within its length [*See Figure 2 and 2(a)*].

3(c) Electrophoresis:

Once the DNA has been digested into RFLPs, the scientist must separate and sort the RFLPs in order to measure them. This is accomplished by gel electrophoresis. In this process, an agarose gel—a gelatin-like substance—is charged with a weak electric field, positive at one end and negative at the other. The RFLPs are then loaded into the negative end, and because DNA has a net negative electrical charge, they flow toward the positive end of the gel. The agarose gel is typically about 18 centimeters long but can be 21 centimeters, and the length varies from lab to lab. All gels are full of holes of varying length, however. As a result, the fragments of DNA become trapped along the way as they try to reach the end of the gel. The longer RFLPs being less flexible and agile tend to get caught early (or at the top of the gel), and the shorter, more agile RFLPs tend to get closer to the positive charge (or the bottom of the gel). The process is something like trying to pull strands of spaghetti through a series of sieves. The longer ones will become entangled first and the shorter strands will become entangled last. Once the DNA strands have been caught, they can be sorted by length and measured[*See Figure 3*].

3(d) Ethidium Bromide Staining:

To mark the RFLPs for further measurement, some laboratories treat the entire gel with Ethidium Bromide. This chemical allows the lanes of DNA to be photographed under ultraviolet light. The ethidium bromide process has been criticized as tending to induce band shifting.[15] See e.g. *People v. Mohit*, 153 Misc.2d 22 (Co. Ct. West Co. 1992). It was also the subject of discussion in the April 1992 report of the National Academy of Science's Committee on DNA Technology in Forensic Science (hereafter "NRC 1992

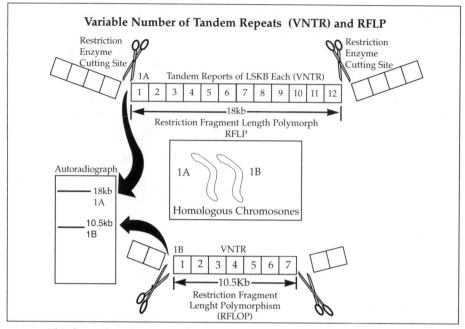

Figure 2 This figure demonstrates RFLP and VNTRs. Alleles (1A and 1B) at a specific locus on a pair of chromosomes. Allele 1A consists of 12 tandem repeats. Allele 1B consists of 7 tandem repeats. The restriction enzyme has generated restriction fragment length polymorphisms of 18-kb (1A) and 10.5-kb (1B).

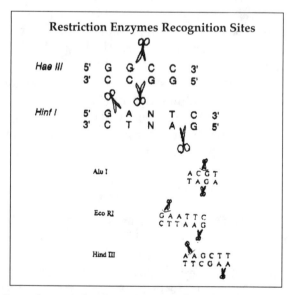

Figure 2 (a) This figure demonstrates the sequences and cutting sites recognized by the noted restriction enzymes. Note the difference where the enzyme cuts the DNA at the same site (HAE 111 and Alu 1) and the staggered sites (HINF 1 and HIND 111).

Genetic Fingerprinting:

Report"), which strongly recommended that the gel be stained with ethidium bromide *after* electrophoresis because this eliminates band shift due to ethidum bromide. Also, staining after electrophoresis requires smaller amounts of ethidium bromide, and that is preferable because the dye is a known carcinogen and thus poses problems of exposure and disposal. The FBI continues to treat their gels with ethidium bromide *before* electrophoresis. However, they report no adverse effects. Their laboratory protocol, dated December 7, 1990, contains this recommended procedure on page 12. Accordingly, if ethidium bromide

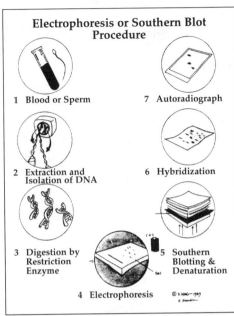

Figure 3

is used, direct and cross examination may explore this issue because it may be important to determine if it is used before or after electrophoresis, and the effect of this election, if any.

3(e) Denaturation and Blotting:

After the RFLPs have been stained for recognition, they are then denatured. This is done through a chemical process or by heating the DNA. Both procedures split the fragments of the DNA molecule into two separate strands, so that each purine is forever divorced from its pyrimidine. (See *Figure 4*) Thus, rather than looking connected like

A C T G

T G A C

the DNA under examination now looks like

A C T G

       T G A C

These single strands are then transferred from the soft malleable gel surface and secured onto the firm surface of a nylon membrane. Now the

RFLPs are fixed in their respective positions so that they can be identified and measured. This is similar to a blotter soaking up an ink stain.

3(f) Hybridization:

Hybridization marks the single strand for measurement. To do this, the scientist utilizes a P-32 radioactively marked probe (P standing for phosphorous), which recognizes a specific DNA sequence. These probes, which consist of single strands of DNA, are contained in solutions into which the membrane is inserted. If, for example, the probe DNA sequence is ACTG, it will find and bind to the TGAC sequence contained on the membrane. If there is no such sequence on the membrane, it will bind with nothing [*See Figure 4*].

The place where the probe binds to the DNA is known as a locus, or loci if there are more than one binding location. Each is numbered according to a standard procedure in which the chromosome DNA is identified. Where the locus is found is preceded by "D" (DNA) and the location on that chromosome is identified by "S" and then a number. For example, the location D2S44 refers to the 44th locus identified on the second chromosome, and D17S79 refers to the 79th locus identified on the 17th chromosome. "D" stands for DNA. The actual ATGC sequence for each locus is known and is stored in a computer maintained by the Human Genome Mapping Project, located at Yale University. Dr. Kenneth K. Kidd, Department of Genetics, Yale University School of Medicine, was the scientist in charge of that project.

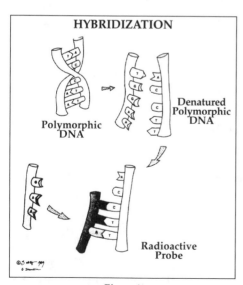

HYBRIDIZATION

Polymorphic DNA

Denatured Polymorphic DNA

Radioactive Probe

Figure 4

Different laboratories use probes that examine different loci. For example, the FBI and Lifecodes examine either D1S7, D4S139, D5S110, D10S28, D14S13, D18S27, DYZ1, DXYS14, D2S44 and D17S79.[16]

Laboratory procedures also vary. For example, unlike the FBI and Lifecodes, who use single locus probes, Cellmark also uses the multi-locus, minisatellite probes developed by Alex Jeffrys in Great Britain which examine several loci at the same time.[17] Cellmark allows the DNA fragments which fall below 2KB to run off the end of its gels in order to maximize its ability to measure and compare the middle range of fragments. Thus, this laboratory does not consider bands weighing less than 2KB in determining whether the known sample matches the forensic sample.

After a sufficient immersion period which varies with the nature of the probe, the membrane is removed and photographed. This process can be repeated by washing the membrane chemically to remove the previous probe and then rehybridizing it with another probe.

3(g)   Creation of the Autoradiograph:

After the radioactively marked membrane is removed from the hybridization solution, it is placed on a piece of x-ray film and exposed for a variable period of time. The combination of ethidium bromide and P-32 now produces an image of the lane of DNA with different alleles radioactively enhanced and visible. The final product looks a little bit like the bar codes on merchandise labels. The marked alleles can now be sized using an electronic computerized digitizing tablet or a lazar process and the measurements compared. If two lanes of samples show bands of DNA at the same site on the membrane, the scientist can conclude that DNA in both lanes came from the same individual. If the measurements differ, the DNA must have come from different individuals. The FBI uses known lengths of DNA for its marker lanes created out of viral DNA. The top band of DNA in the marker lane measures 23,000 KB. The third band from the top marks 10,000 KB. The third band up from the bottom marks 1,000 KB. However, the FBI does not score bands above 10,000 KB or below 1,000 KB based on policy decisions. However, they will consider bands above and below the indicated markers to confirm their opinion of a match.

For HAE 111 digested DNA, the FBI expects their markers on the human control lane composed of the human cell line known as K562, to fall within the following KB (one thousand base pair) locations on their gel:

LOCUS	BAND	MIN.	MAX.
D2S44	1	2893	2981
	2	1785	1839
D17S79	1	1974	2034
	2	1510	1567

LOCUS	BAND	MIN.	MAX.
D1S7	1	4500	4638
	2	4144	4270
D4S139	1	6462	6658
	2	3398	3502
D10S28	1	1739	6658
	2	1178	1213
D5S110	1	3736	3850
	2	2953	3043

The following example illustrates how the autorad works and how the scientist reads it. Assume that blood has been recovered from the scene of a homicide, in which V has been murdered, and that there are three suspects: A, B and C. All have blood stains on their clothes which are being tested. The scientist wishes to compare the victim's blood with the blood stains on their clothes by looking for two alleles, which I will call "Greg" and "Adam." The DNA for V and for the blood stains from A, B, and C will differ in the number of VNTRs and, in schematic form, look like this:

```
V: —Greg [VNTR] [VNTR] Adam————————
A: —-[VNTR] Greg [VNTR] Adam————————
B: —Greg [VNTR] [VNTR] Adam————————
C: —-[VNTR] [VNTR] Greg [VNTR] Adam——
```

Remember that the shorter portions of the cut DNA run to the bottom of the gel and that the longer portions stay nearer the top. The gel contains a marker lane (ML) of known DNA on three sides so the scientist can measure how far each allele traveled on the gel. Thus the autorad will look something like this:

```
ML    V      A     ML    B      C     ML
1                   1           Adam   1
2    Adam   Adam    2   Adam           2
3           Greg    3           Greg   3
4    Greg           4   Greg           4
```

The autorad shows that the blood stain on B's clothes matches the victim's blood. It is the only stain that matches at both "Greg" and "Adam."

4 The Polymerase Chain Reaction:

The second major scientific tool for analysis of forensic DNA samples is the Polymerase Chain Reaction, or PCR. This method was first used in casework in 1986, but the system for using it was not widely available until 1990. PCR is an enzymatic process by which a specific region of DNA is replicated over and over to yield several million copies of a particular sequence. The area of the genome that is currently used most frequently is the DQ-Alpha region of the Human Leukocyte Antigen, found on the sixth chromosome,[18] but as of 1993 some ten regions of the genome have been discussed in the scientific literature as appropriate for PCR analysis.[19] Two commercial PCR analysis kits are used most frequently in forensic laboratories: the DQ Alpha Amplitype Kit[20] produced by Cetus Corporation, and the AmpliType PM (also known as the Polymarker)[21] produced by Roche Molecular Systems.[22] All are trademarked. The techniques employed by all three are substantially the same; thus, rather than needlessly prolonging the necessarily technical discussion that follows by discussing each possible site for examination, I will focus on the examination of the DQ Alpha locus to explain how the process works. Substantial differences in the techniques pertaining to other loci will be noted in footnotes [*See Figure 4(a)*].

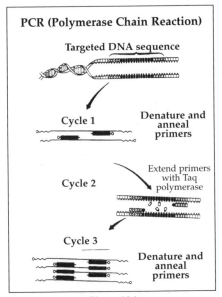

PCR (Polymerase Chain Reaction)

Targeted DNA sequence

Cycle 1 — Denature and anneal primers

Cycle 2 — Extend primers with Taq polymerase

Cycle 3 — Denature and anneal primers

Figure 4(a)

The DQ Alpha[23] region consists of 242 base pairs and contains ten alleles. The DQ Alpha Amplitype Kit recognizes six of these alleles (known as: 1.1, 1.2, 1.3, 2, 3, and 4), which can appear in various combinations and form a total of twenty-one genetic types. Type 4 is sub-divided into three alleles, known as 4.1, 4.2, and 4.3. 4.1 can be easily distinguished from the other subtypes, but 4.2 and 4.3 are relatively rare and, in the sequence targeted by this kit, they are identical. Thus, these alleles are not revealed by this kit. The other two alleles are variations of the 3 allele which have only recently been identified (1994). They are so rare that, so far, they have been observed in less than one hundred humans and are not yet examined by the kit.

During the PCR process, DNA is denatured, or unzipped, by a heat process (94 degrees C for one minute) and oriented so that the 3'ends[24] of each strand point toward each other. The temperature is then lowered (60 degrees C) and oligonucleotide primers[25] and elemental DNA building blocks[26] are introduced into the solution. These primers identify the two ends of the region of the DQ Alpha locus and provide guideposts for where the process is to start. Then an enzyme known as Taq, isolated from the bacterium *Thermus aquaticus*,[27] is introduced and the temperature is raised again (72 degrees C) causing the enzyme to extend the primers across the region in a template directed manner,[28] picking up the elemental building blocks as they go, so that the building blocks bind to their complementary A, T, C, or G on each strand of the unzipped DNA and form two separate, identical strands of new DNA. This process is then repeated to create four new strands, eight new strands, sixteen new strands, and so forth over thirty-two cycles, resulting in about 10 billion new strands of DQ Alpha, each of which is identical to that contained in the forensic sample.[29] In essence, this process is the same that our bodies use to replicate our cells and that we used to grow from a zygote in our mother's womb to a full grown adult.

After the PCR process has been completed, the scientist must identify what alleles are present. This is done by a dot blot assay, unlike RFLP analysis where the DNA is attached to a membrane which is then dipped into a solution containing the identifying probes.[30] In the currently available PCR kits all the probes are contained on a membrane which is dipped into the solution containing the amplified DNA. The alleles which are present then bind to the area of the membrane that contains their complimentary probe and cause a blue dot[31] to form at the portion of the membrane that identifies the particular allele identified. The typical membrane used for DQ Alpha analysis contains nine probes which are identified as: 1; 2; 3; 4; C (control); 1.1, 1.2, 1.3. The advantage of this system is that all probes may be hybridized in just one dipping. The scientist then compares the dots from the forensic sample to the dots from the defendant's blood sample. If they are the same, we have a match; if they differ, we have an exclusion. Dots that are less intense than the control dot, i.e., not as blue, are not counted. If the process for those alleles did not work at least as well as it did for the control, the scientist cannot be sure that they actually represent DNA or that they accurately reflect which allele they bound to. If none of the dots are as bright as the control, the result is inconclusive.

PCR also differs from RFLP in that the DNA is not cut into pieces by a restriction enzyme during analysis. Rather the process works by identifying the area of interest by the two oglionucleotide primers that attach at either end of the target area. Both primers are about 18-20 base pairs in length and differ in the order of the base pairs. Thus, a highly specific area of the genome can be targeted. In the case of DQ Alpha, which codes for a protein that is unique to that locus (i.e., no other portion of the entire genome can produce this protein), the scientists found the appropriate sequence for the primers to target by mapping the 242-base-pair-portion of the genome that comprises the DQ Alpha locus and then by mapping the 18 base pairs on each side of that locus. Thus these primers will target just that single portion of the entire genome. Then during the PCR process only the DQ Alpha region is amplified. The rest of the DNA just sits there and does nothing. Thus, after thirty amplification cycles the final product contains 10 billion copies of DQ Alpha and just one of everything else which has not been affected by the process. The membrane containing probes that identify just the DQ Alpha alleles is then dipped into this lopsided mixture and the result is read. Thus, as you can see, the test reveals just the DQ Alpha and not the rest of the genome. You can think of the rest of the genome as a single grain of black sand that has a whole truckload of white sand dumped on it. Thus a shovel of sand taken from the top of the pile will reveal only white sand.

The advantage of PCR is that it can be used to examine minute quantities of DNA. RFLP analysis requires, ideally, between 1 to 2.5 micrograms of high molecular weight DNA (i.e., 21 KB or more)[32] to obtain a good pattern. This means that the scientist should be presented with 50 to 100 microliters of blood or semen and at least 15 hairs with intact roots. Blood contains 5,000 to 10,000 nucleated cells per microliter; this corresponds to 25-50 micrograms of DNA per microliter. Semen analysis requires 10 microliters. PCR analysis, on the other hand, can be performed on 2 nanograms or less[33] of DNA. Thus a single hair with an intact root or the saliva found on a cigarette butt or an envelope or stamp can produce enough DNA for analysis. The scientists estimate that as little as 100 cells will provide sufficient DNA for successful PCR replication. Nonetheless, this method will work only if there is an intact stretch of DNA between the two sites where the oligonucleotide primers attach to the denatured DNA. Following the amplification process, gel electrophoresis should be employed, using six microliters of each control and each sample to determine whether the process worked correctly.[34] The protocols for the Amplitype Kit state that after electrophoresis the following six bands should clearly appear in the control lane: 242/239 bp (DQ Alpha); 214 bp (LDLR); 190 bp (GYPA); 172 bp (HBGG); 151 bp (D7S8) and 138 bp (GC). The DNA should not be heat denatured prior to electrophoresis; it may cause additional bands to appear, or it may cause bands to smear. There could be direct or cross examination on this issue.

PCR is the preferred analysis when the forensic sample contains DNA that has been degraded, i.e., eaten by bacteria. As long as the bacteria has eaten DNA that is not located at DQ-Alpha (a common occurrence since DNA is 3 billion base pairs long and DQ-Alpha comprises just 242 base pairs of that length), this PCR kit will generate a result. As long as the average size of the degraded fragments is longer than the target size, i.e., 243 base pairs or longer, PCR analysis should be considered. In fact Cetus Laboratory has noted that slightly degraded DNA sometimes allows for greater yields of PCR generated DNA than occur with DNA samples of molecular weight. They theorize that slightly degraded DNA denatures more easily and thus binds to more primers during the first stages of amplification.[35] RFLP, which examines much longer portions of the molecule, has much less chance of success when the forensic sample is degraded. PCR DQ Alpha analysis is impossible after DNA has been digested by HAE 111 because HAE 111 digestion destroys the recognition site for the PCR process. Therefore, if a sufficient sample is available to perform both RFLP and PCR, the sample should be separated before either analysis is conducted. Another advantage is that the process can be repeated for as long as necessary. Thus, in theory, an unlimited amount of forensic DNA can be available for reanalysis by another laboratory.[36]

There are two major disadvantages to the PCR technology. The first is that the process works indiscriminately in the sense that it will amplify all of the DNA that it identifies during the procedure. Thus, if DNA from another specimen is mixed with the forensic sample by mistake, that DNA's DQ-Alpha will be amplified along with the DQ-Alpha of the forensic sample with the result that more alleles may appear on the dot blot assay than are actually present in the forensic sample. Careful laboratory procedures can be employed to minimize the risk that more than one DNA will be amplified, but that risk remains nonetheless.[37] Direct and cross-examination will probably be directed at the notion that laboratory error did or did not cause contamination during the PCR process; thus the laboratory should be prepared to present their laboratory's protocols and lab notes to show that the tests were performed properly.

The second disadvantage to the PCR process lies in the fact that the DQ-Alpha process has the capacity to identify just twenty-one separate alleles, as opposed to the many thousands of alleles that can be identified through RFLP analysis. Thus, it is less powerful evidence in the event of a match.[38] For this reason, PCR is most useful as a tool for excluding a suspect as the source of the forensic sample. There have been instances where a person has been included in PCR DQ-Alpha testing and subsequently excluded when PCR Polymarkers and RFLP testing was conducted.

5   Special Problems Attending Forensic Application of DNA Identification Technology:

5(a)   RFLP:

When scientists use Southern Blots for chemical or diagnostic purposes, they use fresh or dried blood samples from a known source. Thus, if a particular experiment gives an uninterpretable result, the scientist need only obtain more blood from the patient and repeat the experiment. In forensic cases, however, the sample—say a blood stain found at a crime scene or a semen sample obtained from a rape victim—is limited. If the experiment goes awry, there is no way to redo it. Thus, for forensic purposes there is only one bite at the apple, and the forensic scientist must take special pains to be sure that the experiment has proper controls which ensure that it was performed correctly. (See *People v. Castro, infra.*) Additionally, forensic samples are frequently contaminated by material which mixes with the blood at the scene, or by bacteria which grow in the sample. If these contaminants contain DNA, that DNA will show on the autoradiograph along with the human DNA. Thus, the forensic scientist must also have a method for determining which DNA is which. (See *People v. Castro, infra.*) Other factors that affect the quality of the sample and the potential reliability of the evidence of a match or an exclusion are the age of the forensic sample and the conditions to which it has been exposed. Heat, drying, high humidity, and ultra violet radiation through sunlight are common environmental insults that can affect the quality of the forensic sample.

Unlike the clinical scientist who can simply obtain more sample which is uncontaminated, the forensic scientist must make the best interpretation possible with what is available. If the forensic sample is, to some degree, of lesser quality than a whole blood sample taken at a hospital, the forensic scientist's interpretation of the results may, to that degree, be suspect. Expect direct and cross-examination to focus on this point.

Other potential problems that can effect the reliability of each step of the RFLP process abound. For example, if the DNA is degraded—that is eaten by bacteria, or exposed to enzymes that cause the same effect, the operation of the restriction enzyme may be affected. For example, HAE 111 recognizes the sequence GGCC and cuts the DNA between the G and the C [*See Figure 2(b)*]. If any of the Gs or Cs happen to be the nucleotide(s) that the bacterium ate, HAE 111 will skip the site. The result is a fragment that is longer than it should be. This in turn will result in a given band appearing higher in the gel than it should, and if this anomaly is not recognized for what it is, the result will probably be a false exclusion.

"Partial Digestion" causes a similar problem. This results when a restriction enzyme does not cut the DNA as often as it should because of degradation, contamination or mutation. The experienced forensic scientist should be capable of recognizing and explaining the phenomenon of partial digestion from the location where the anomalous bands appear on the autorad. For example, in a murder case presented in July, 1995, the FBI reported the following data regarding partial digestion of fragments in its gels. The expert cautioned that the sizes are approximate and reflect the difference between primary fragments. These differences represent the estimated number of base pairs between the two sites cut by HAE 111 on either side of the locus being examined. The sizes underlined reflects the side which experiences partial digestion most often. The third number reflects the fragment size that occurs when there is extensive partial digestion which is referred to as "partialing". This occurs when the restriction enzyme misses both cuts that flank the locus being examined:

LOCUS   ESTIMATED SIZES

D2S44   550, 1730, 2280
D17S79   100, 200
D1S7   200, 400, 600 (no partialing where fragments large or when only small partialing with other probes.)
D4S139   None noticed in casework.
D10S28   260, 1330, 1590
D5S110   160, 320, 480 (little partialing noted)

The gel itself, as a second example, can, in spots, vary in thickness, consistency, and temperature. These differences can cause band shifting. The voltage used to draw the DNA down through the gel can fluctuate, again causing band shifting. *[See Figure 5(a) pg. 72]*

A third area that may be the focus of direct or cross examination is the Southern blotting process: here the transfer of the DNA from the gel to the nylon membrane may be imprecise, effectively smearing the results; or a bubble on the membrane can block the transfer of the DNA causing some bands to disappear. In short, you should be aware of each step of the process in order to follow the direct and cross examination of the experts.

The forensic scientist also faces problems in interpreting the autoradiograph which clinical scientists do not. The clinical scientist knows who the subject is and can obtain blood samples from the subject's parents. Thus, the clinical scientist can run lanes of the subject's parents' DNA alongside that of the subject. This procedure allows for relative certainty in measuring the kilo-base size of a given allele.

Since the allele in question must have been transmitted to the subject by one of the parents, a comparison of the three DNA samples can resolve ambiguities about whether one allele in fact matches another. The forensic scientist does not have this luxury. The forensic sample comes from an unknown source whose parent can be anybody in the world. Thus, of necessity, the forensic scientist's opinion must be more subjective than that of the clinical scientist. Expect this point to be explored on direct and cross examination.

5(b) PCR:

Potential problems also plague the polymerase chain reaction. Those that are common to both PCR and RFLP analysis include operator carelessness, inappropriate application and poor reagents. Others, however, are peculiar to PCR. The most important is sample contamination.

Sample contamination usually occurs in one of four ways. First the sample can be contaminated at the crime scene: a sneeze by one of the crime scene detectives or the ADA on homicide duty can be enough to do it; a scratch of the head causing dandruff or other dead skin cells to fall into a sample is another common source of contamination. The scientists say that, at the recommended sensitivity levels contained in the protocols for DQ Alpha analysis, the danger of a sneeze as a source of contamination is negligible. The scratch of the head is another matter, however. Second, and more common—especially in sex cases—the forensic sample may contain a mixture of fluids from more than one person. When the mixture contains intact sperm heads, the problem diminishes because sperm heads can be isolated, as previously noted. Mixed blood, mixed saliva, mixed blood and saliva, or mixed sperm samples from a multiple rape cannot be separated as easily. This point may be developed on direct or cross examination. However, it may also be noted that the medical use of PCR technology also works on mixed and contaminated samples. The example of amniocentesis may be used as the cells of the mother and fetus are extracted, amplified and examined.

Further examples may include the extraction of cancer or HIV-infected cells where the entire point of the test is to identify the few diseased cells hidden within a large population of healthy cells. Also, PCR is used in the detection of HIV in discarded needles. Thus, where there is a mixture of fluids, such as blood, saliva and sperm, a prosecutor should think long and hard before authorizing PCR analysis. The wrong decision can create *Brady* material, whether spurious or not. From the defense end, such mixtures can easily create a false exclusion. (See *California v. McSherry, infra.*) A further source for other ideas in this area is contained in McKnight, *The Polymerase Chain Reaction (PCR): The Second Generation of DNA Analysis Methods Takes The Stand,* 9 Computer and High Technology Law Journal 314 (1993).

The third common source of contamination is the exposure of the sample to another strain of human DNA at the laboratory through poor pipette procedure or the mixing of test tube caps from one sample to the next.[39] This is especially fatal since there is no way to obtain a fresh source for the forensic sample.[40]

The fourth common source is carryover of PCR enhanced DNA from one analysis to the next. Any of these can result in a false exclusion because alleles from a stranger will appear to be those of the suspect.[41] If the test results in an unbelievable exclusion, in a date-rape case for example, there should arise suspicions that laboratory contamination may be the cause. This source of a false exclusion is particularly probable when the forensic sample contains foreign alleles in addition to alleles that match the defendant's alleles. Contamination is revealed most frequently by the presence of more than two alleles.[42]

Other problems may cause the polymerase Taq to malfunction. Certain components in blue denim and some leathers inhibit the process; blood stains recovered from leaves and some soil samples have failed to amplify as they should; and some old blood stains release a heme-containing[43] component upon extraction that also inhibits the process. These problems can be eliminated by adding more Taq and primers to the amplification mixture.

More potential problems arise during the amplification process. Temperature is crucial in the denaturing process because some alleles unzip at different temperatures than others. For example, Dr. Edward Blake has observed that, at 88-89 degrees C, the 4 allele will denature, but the 1 allele will not. This may be due to the fact that the 1 allele has a higher G/C content relative to the 2, 3, and 4 alleles.[44] If the DNA does not denature, the PCR primers cannot anneal to it and that portion of the sample will not amplify. A bogus conclusion results. This problem can be detected by use of a control sample that contains the 2, 3, 4 and one of the 1 alleles. Thus if all those alleles are not amplified, the scientist can determine that something may be wrong in the denaturing process of the forensic sample. Temperature is equally important in amplification process: if the temperature is too high, annealing is prohibited; if it is too low, the annealing is non-specific and reduces the yield of the DNA under examination. The same is true for the hybridization of the DNA to the probe; the DQ Alpha test has a two degree temperature window that must be maintained if the test is to be successful. For this reason all PCR equipment should be calibrated using a Temperature Verification System (a part for the machine supplied by the manufacturer) at least once a month. The timing of the various cycles is also important. Each step of PCR process should be completed within precise time limitations[45] to minimize the formation of extraneous materials and non-specific PCR products.

Environmental insult and degradation, especially in the form of prolonged exposure to sunlight, also can affect the PCR process. If the degradation has caused the DNA to break into fragments that are smaller than the area of the genome to be amplified, the process will not work. Moreover, badly degraded DNA can cause incompletely extended portions of the DNA to jump from one template to the other, resulting in a bogus amplified product.[46] Finally, there is the potential for mutation during the PCR process by expanding sequence errors, that is by picking up an extra A, T, C, or G by mistake through chemical magnetism or dropping one by mistake.[47] This too results in a bogus final product.

It should be stressed that the last two examples of potential error are highly unlikely, but as we all know, strange things can occur during the trial of a DNA case. (See *People v. Castro, infra.*) The experts should be prepared to discuss this type of problem on direct or cross examination. The experts must be able to explain away these problems on the basis of statistics and data generated at their laboratory.

Finally, the dot blot assay membrane (the strip with the blue dots that allows the scientist to interpret the results) is subject to discoloration over time. As a result, it should be photographed while wet to preserve a permanent record of the results. This is important because the intensity of the alleles present is gauged by how blue the dots are. Dots that are insufficiently intense may be discounted as genuine alleles. Thus when the opponent's expert examines the membrane in court the expert may argue that certain dots should be discounted. The photograph will allow the expert to effectively meet this line of attack. It undoubtedly can also be extremely helpful to the court and jury in understanding the issue.

6 TWGDAM and ASCLD:

Two organizations have addressed the types of problems peculiar to forensic DNA analysis. The first was formed under the auspices of the FBI and consists of a group of respected scientists known (in classic federal bureaucratese) as "Technical Working Group on DNA Analysis Methods" or TWGDAM. In association with the California Association of Criminalist Ad Hoc Committee on DNA Quality Assurance, TWGDAM has prepared a pamphlet entitled *Guidelines for a Quality Assurance Program for DNA Analysis*. Most forensic scientists and virtually all courts regard the TWG-DAM guidelines as the state-of-the-art, up-to-the-minute standard for forensic DNA analysis. The second group is the American Society of Crime

Laboratory Directors (ASCLD), which has added a section on DNA analysis to their Laboratory Accreditation Board Manual. In it they set forth standards for proficiency tests which all forensic scientists that I know accept as state-of-the-art. For a crime laboratory, attaining ASCLD accreditation is roughly the equivalent of a lawyer passing the Bar Examination. Avoiding detail as much as possible, set forth is the general suggested guidelines.

TWGDAM starts by setting forth qualifications for laboratory personnel. A supervisor/technical leader should have:

(1) a minimum of a BA/BS or its equivalent in a biological, chemical or forensic science and have received credit in courses in genetics, biochemistry and molecular biology (molecular genetics, recombinant DNA technology) or other subjects which provide a basic understanding of the foundation of forensic DNA analysis

(2) documented training in DNA analysis in a program that included methods, equipment, procedures, and materials used in forensic DNA analysis and their applications and limitations

(3) two years experience as a forensic biology examiner; and

(4) stay abreast of the developments in the field by reading current scientific literature, attending seminars, and so forth

Examiner/Analysts must have a minimum of a BS/BA or its equivalent, one year of forensic biology experience, and six months experience in a DNA laboratory before doing actual case work. Technicians should have a minimum of a BS/BA or equivalent and receive on-the-job training by a qualified analyst. Technicians will not interpret DNA typing results, prepare final reports or provide testimony concerning these matters.

TWGDAM also recommends a series of evidence handling procedures to ensure a valid chain of evidence and guard against outside contamination and a list of procedures by which outside labs may ensure that the probes used specifically target the sequence that they are intended to identify and that the loci identified are on file at the Yale Gene library. I have omitted detailed discussion because, as of March 1993, as far as I know, all labs that are in business have complied with the validation procedures and there is little likelihood that cross examination will be fruitful in this area.

Direct and cross examination, however, will likely focus on those portions of the TWGDAM guidelines which suggest analytical procedures. This area is highly technical and difficult to understand at first, but it should become comprehensible after a second or third reading. I include some detail because each of these controls should be in place in the expert's lab and you will need to know about them to make sure that that you understand the issue so that there will be no unexpected surprises (which may cause unpleasant discomfort) for you on direct and cross examination.

As a general rule, TWGDAM guidelines provide that samples should be tested in ways that provide maximum information with the least consumption of the sample, and that whenever possible, a portion of the sample should either be retained by the laboratory or returned to the submitting agency. When a semen sample is to be identified, a differential extraction should be employed; that is, a step-by-step extraction procedure that separates intact sperm heads from lysed sperm and from other, e.g., epithelial, cell types. This separation generally will result in an enrichment of sperm DNA in one cell fraction relative to the others. Each can be analyzed individually. The isolation procedure for removing the DNA from the rest of the cell should protect against sample contamination, and the effectiveness of the procedure should be evaluated by regular use of known source of human DNA (usually Hela, a commercially available known DNA or a sample from one of the laboratory personnel).

Once the DNA has been isolated, a procedure should be used to estimate the quality (extent of DNA degradation) and quantity of DNA recovered from the specimen. This step is important because DNA can degrade randomly (the bacteria may eat any portion of the molecule). If DNA is degraded at the high end of the molecular weight spectrum, then when it is cut by the restriction enzyme, the pieces of DNA will be shorter than they should be and will run to the lower part of the analytical gel. Thus, if a probe that identifies D2S44 (which is seen at 10KB and above) is used, that probe will light up on the sample of the suspect's blood but not on the forensic sample because that portion of the DNA is missing. The result is a false exclusion. Thus the scientist must determine whether RFLP (and, if so, which probes) or PCR is the appropriate testing method before the sample is consumed. Recommended methods include:

(1) a yield gel that includes a set of high molecular weight
     calibration standards by which to measure the sample
     (i.e., a lane of known human DNA)
(2) ultra violet absorption against known DNA
(3) fluorescence against known concentrations of high
     molecular weight DNA
(4) hybridization, against known standards, with a specific (ideally
     monomorphic) probe that identifies high molecular weight DNA

Recommended analytical procedures for RFLP analysis include requirements for both the restriction enzymes and the analytical gel. Prior to its initial use, each batch of restriction enzymes (which can either be pur-chased or home-grown in the laboratory) should be tested against known DNA under standard conditions. If the expected pattern is revealed in the known standard, the scientist knows that the restriction enzyme is working properly in the abstract. To determine whether the restriction enzyme operated properly in the case at hand, a test gel should be used which includes size markers (i.e., known lanes of DNA) and human DNA control lane which measures the effectiveness of the digestion. If all appears prop-er, the scientist knows that the forensic DNA has been cut at the proper places on the genome.[48]

The analytical gel used to separate the restriction fragments MUST include the following:

(1) visual or fluorescent markers to determine the end point of electrophoresis
(2) molecular weight size markers which bracket the lanes containing the samples being tested
(3) a human DNA[49] control which produces a known pattern with each probe used and serves as an internal systems check for the following functions—
  (a) electrophoresis quality and resolution [Is the gel itself O.K.?]
  (b) sizing process [Did the electrophoresis cause the DNA to stretch out enough so that each allele can be separately identified and measured? i.e., is the apparent homozygous band really homozygous or do two heterozygous bands appear as one because the DNA has not separated properly?]
  (c) probe identity [Does the pattern look the way that it should?]
  (d) hybridization efficiency [Do the patterns show over the whole length of the gel in the way that they should?];
  (e) stripping efficiency [Did all of the probe used in the prior hybridization get washed off the membrane before this test was conducted? i.e., am I looking at leftover DNA loci from the last probe in addition to the loci I should be seeing with this probe?]

One human DNA control that should be included is named K 562. This is a known cell line which is recognized as valid by the scientific com-munity. It is supposed to be used in every lab in the country so that the results may be compared to national data published by the National Institute of Standards and Technology. Obviously, if the results for K 562 on the expert's autorad correspond to those achieved by other labs across the country, that represents solid and powerful evidence that the expert per-

Genetic Fingerprinting:

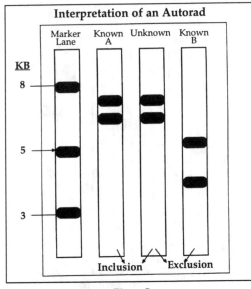

Interpretation of an Autorad

Figure 5

formed the test properly [*See Figure 5*].

Additionally, TWGDAM states that a procedure should be available to interpret altered migration of DNA fragments. This refers to artifacts or band shift. An artifact is something that appears on an autorad that is not human DNA. Given the infinite variety of locations on which forensic evidence can be found, e.g., barnyards or fecal stained underwear, an artifact can be almost anything. Common examples include bacterial or vegetable matter. Usually an artifact can be distinguished from a true DNA band by the naked eye, and even lawyers and judges can do it with confidence. But the diagnosis of something as an artifact (that can be disregarded for identification purposes) is a matter of interpretation about which experts will disagree. If not obviously something other than human DNA, however, an artifact may be an indication that something was wrong in the gel, the restriction enzyme, or the probe. If an artifact is mistakenly interpreted as a true band, the result is a false inclusion or exclusion. (See *People v. Castro, infra.*) [*See Figure 5(a)*].

Band shift, as the name implies, refers to a phenomenon in which two (or more) lanes of DNA run at different speeds through the gel during electrophoresis which causes them to "shift" and to appear at different places on the gel with respect to each other and to the marker lanes than they should. Band shift is caused by the fact that the DNA is pulled through a gel that is primarily made of water and which contains some salt. Both elements are affected by factors including barometric pressure, humidity, temperature and the like. The result is that the gel offers more resistance at some places than it does at others causing the DNA to run faster or slower than it would under ideal conditions. Thus, for example, a forensic lane will show a band at 7KB and the suspect lane will show a band at 6KB. In fact the bands match, but they appear not to. Conversely, bands that do not match can appear to match with the risk that some innocent person may be falsely identified.[50] For example, blood from a deceased person degrades more quickly that vaginal secretions. Thus, in a recent rape and murder case in New York, the lanes containing the victims blood did not match the lane from her vagina, in an RFLP test. Because the DNA from her post mortem blood had degraded more quickly than the vaginal sample, it was "thinner" than the vaginal sample and ran more quickly through the gel. Nothing can prevent band shift. One can only scientifically and reliably identify it. [*See Figure 5(a), 6 and 7*]

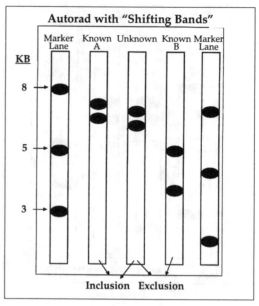

Figure 5(a)

Four methods have been suggested to identify band shift and, no doubt, the experts may testify about others. One method is to run a mixed lane containing both forensic DNA and suspect DNA and place it between the lanes of forensic DNA and suspect DNA. The mixed lane will show all of the bands that appear on both lanes, and since there is but one lane, band shift will remain constant for both samples within it. If all the bands on the mixed lane match all the bands on the other lanes, the scientist knows that band shift did not occur.

The second method is the "internal molecular weight standard", that is, using monomorphic probes which bracket the area of interest. A hypothetical example illustrates the point: If a scientist wishes to examine lanes A and B in the area at D17S79, which shows bands in the 2-4KB range, the scientist would use monomorphic probes which identify bands at 1KB and 6KB. Thus, if the D17S79 band in lane A appears at 5KB and the monomorphic probes appear at 2KB and 7KB, the scientist knows that the gel ran slowly and that the 5KB band at D17S79 is a true band rather than an artifact. And, if the monomorphic probes in lane B appear at 1KB and 5KB the scientist knows that lane B ran relatively fast. Thus, hypothetically, the scientist could decide that the 5KB band in lane A matches a 4KB band in lane B. If this method is used, the scientist should use monomorphic probes which bracket both sides of every diagnostic probe employed. The April, 1992 Report endorses this method.

The third method is simply to clean the samples (by re-extraction, dialy-

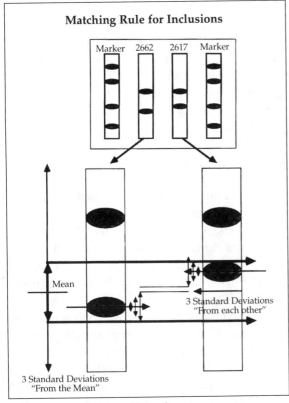

Figure 6

sis, or other measures) and to rehybridize and create another autorad. In the past, Lifecodes has used this method. As a scientific matter there is nothing wrong with this method, and it is also endorsed by the April, 1992 Report. But, this approach can create a problem for the judge in understanding the process. The adversary can argue that the first, or band-shifted gel was correct and that the second gel displays band shift, creating what may be needless controversy for resolution by the court. The mixed lane approach overcomes this objection and should be used if there is sufficient forensic sample to do so.

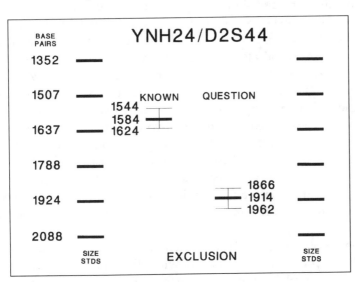

Figure 7

The fourth method is to see if there is streaking on the autorad. This is often evidence of degradation and can cause band shifting. Where band shift is present, the April, 1992 Report recommends a policy that all laboratories report that the results are inconclusive. This is not binding on the court if the scientific explanation warrants a different conclusion.

With regard to determining whether two bands on different lanes match, TWGDAM endorses visual observation but requires confirmation by quantitative analysis that is computerized or lazar measurement that demonstrates that both bands fall within the laboratory's match criteria. (See figure 6)

For PCR analysis TWGDAM requires two negative controls with each sample: a reagent blank and an amplification blank. The reagent blank control consists of all reagents (enzymes, oligonucleotides, solutions etc.) minus any sample. It is used to detect any DNA that may be present in the analytical reagents and materials. (Remember PCR indiscriminately amplifies all DNA that is present. If this control shows positive, the scientist knows that the amplified DNA has come from more than one source.) The amplification blank consists of the amplification reagents without the sample DNA and works in the same fashion as the reagent blank.

Other controls include the addition of known human DNA at the amplification step as a positive control to be carried through the remainder of the typing. The assumption here is that if the known DNA performs as expected the forensic sample must have produced the proper result. TWGDAM also recommends that, where appropriate, substrate controls should be collected from the evidence (e.g., unstained areas adjacent to stained areas, hair shafts adjacent to hair roots) and should be processed at the same time as the forensic samples. This also helps to eliminate the possibility that foreign DNA has been amplified. Where feasible, TWGDAM recommends that the sample should be split for duplicate analysis as early as possible prior to amplification. It also recommends that (where the dot blot assay or the reverse dot blot assay is not used) that markers which span the allele size range be used and that forensic and suspect sample be bracketed by marker lanes.

Finally, TWGDAM requires at least two open proficiency tests and one blind test each year. At this point we move into ASCLD's domain. ASCLD is the body that ensures that each forensic laboratory follows TWGDAM guidelines and is producing acceptable work. ASCLD accreditation extends for five years, and to maintain accreditation, a laboratory must successfully complete two open proficiency tests and at least one blind proficiency test each year.

An open proficiency test occurs when the laboratory knows that is being tested; a blind proficiency test occurs when the laboratory does not know that the "case sample" submitted to it by a police department or District

---

Genetic Fingerprinting:

Attorney's office is in fact an ASCLD designed proficiency test. Proficiency tests are designed by other forensic laboratories and are intended to duplicate actual case work. Thus, unlike a proficiency test designed by the State Department of Health or other agency that regulates "pure science", which consists of samples presented under laboratory standards of cleanliness, an ASCLD designed test, in a sex case for example, will consist of semen on a piece of cloth that in addition contains body grime, epithelial cells, and menstrual blood (none of which necessarily has come from the same woman). In a homicide case, the test might consist of blood which has been thrown on dirty blue jeans which have been left in the basement for a week.

To quote the ASCLD guidelines, "The minimum criteria that must be met in order to demonstrate acceptable performance in a DNA proficiency test are as follows:

1. All DNA Analysis Methods
   (a) All reported matches must be correct.
   (b) All reported non-matches must be correct.
   (c) All results reported as inconclusive or
       uninterpretable must be consistent with the
       documented interpretational guidelines used in case work.

2. RFLP Analysis
   Reported allele sizing data for proficiency samples and cell line controls must agree within plus or minus three standard deviations[51] of the group mean as determined for each locus reported.

3. PCR Product analysis
   Reported genotype(s) for each proficiency
   sample must agree with the target genotype(s)

Test failures fall into three classes: Class I failures, i.e., a false inclusion or false exclusion, which raise immediate concern about the quality of the laboratory's work; Class II failures, i.e., reporting inconclusive results on a sample which most labs identify correctly (these are cause for concern but are not persistent or serious enough to cause immediate concern for the over-all quality of the laboratory's work product); Class III failures, or discrepancies that have minimal effect or significance, will be unlikely to recur, are not systematic and do not significantly affect the fundamental reliability of the laboratory's work.

Class I failures or serious Class II failures, under TWGDAM guidelines,

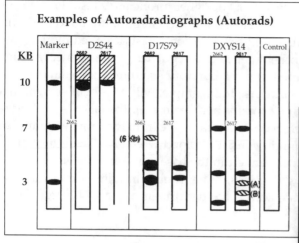

Figure 8

Special Experiments

1. Serial Dilution
2. Mixing Experiments
3. Non-polymorphic Probes
4. Exposure Time
5. Parent's Lane
6. Synthetic Probe

prohibit further examination of actual case evidence by the responsible individuals until the cause of the problem is identified and corrected. Class I failures also may trigger a loss of ASCLD accreditation and require an independent review of all actual case work performed by the laboratory since it last passed a proficiency test. These are suggested guidelines. Adherence to them may or may not affect the reliability of the results [*See Figure 8*].

7 POPULATION GENETICS:

After the autoradiograph in RFLP or the PCR dot blot has been produced, the scientist faces the task of interpreting the results. If the DNA samples match, the question is to determine the likelihood that the match is unique to one individual. This question is answered according to the principles of population genetics. Population Genetics is concerned with the genetics of natural populations, as the name implies. Traditional genetic experiments are performed on animals and plants because controlled mating is possible. In human population studies, the geneticist uses observations and mathematical theories in place of actual experiments on humans. Therefore, observations of the frequency or rareness of different traits (eye color, skin color, body size, heart disease, etc.), genotypes, genes and the repeating variable base pairs between genes (VNTRs) are set forth in a highly developed mathematical theory. This permits the population geneticist to predict and test their predictions.

Fortunately for the judge, lawyer and lay person, only the more elementary aspects of the complicated mathematical theories of population genetics are needed for forensic purposes. This is possible because VNTRs and other molecular markers used in forensic DNA can be measured by standard testing procedures. Complications arising from gene traits and diseases, where inferences about the genes and possible environmental influences must be made, are not involved in the portion of the genome that is utilized in DNA forensic testing.

The population geneticist determines the frequency with which a specific allele occurs within a given human racial group. In the case of common alleles, for example the Rh positive blood types, the frequency of occurrences in the human population is quite large. Thus, if both DNA samples show the Rh positive allele, the population geneticist can say only that both samples could have come from any person, male or female, who is part of the majority of the human population. In the case of the Rh negative allele, the population geneticist can say that the allele is somewhat more rare and that the samples come from a minority of the human population. In the case of alleles (VNTRs) that occur in the anonymous or polymorphic section of the genome, the likelihood that the samples (VNTRs) will match is much smaller. This lesser the likelihood of matches amongst VNTRs is what gives the DNA identification technology its value for forensic purposes.

Population genetics derives its force for identification purposes from the small likelihood that a given anonymous allele will occur randomly in the relevant racial population. For this estimation to be valid, two preconditions must exist. First, the occurrences of the allele must not be caused by linkage disequilibrium, and second, the relevant racial population as a whole must be in Hardy-Weinberg equilibrium.

For these purposes, a population is in equilibrium when the alleles within it occur at the frequency which would exist if the alleles were transmitted from parent to child by chance alone. Thus, when two alleles under examination appear on a single chromosome of the parent, the chance is lessened that the child received both alleles randomly. The reason for this is that when the parent's chromosome splits during mating, there is more chance that alleles on a single chromosome will attach to each other and then become part of the child's genome than would occur if the alleles were located on different chromosomes. Hence, there is less chance that they were transmitted randomly. When this phenomenon occurs, the alleles are linked, and for this allele, the population is in linkage disequilibrium. When the alleles exist on different chromosomes, linkage cannot occur, and the appearance of the allele in the child may be said to have occurred randomly. In this case, the population is not in linkage disequilibrium, (or, stated differently, the population is in linkage equilibrium) and for this reason, each probe used in a forensic case should identify a locus on a different chromosome.

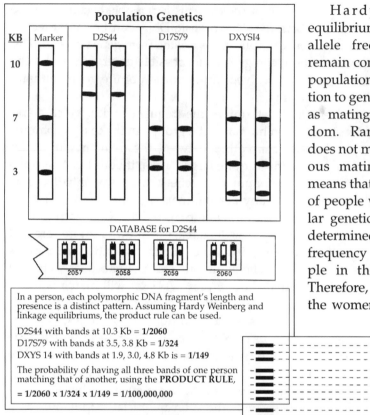

Population Genetics

DATABASE for D2S44

In a person, each polymorphic DNA fragment's length and presence is a distinct pattern. Assuming Hardy Weinberg and linkage equilibriums, the product rule can be used.

D2S44 with bands at 10.3 Kb = **1/2060**
D17S79 with bands at 3.5, 3.8 Kb = **1/324**
DXYS 14 with bands at 1.9, 3.0, 4.8 Kb is = **1/149**

The probability of having all three bands of one person matching that of another, using the **PRODUCT RULE**,

= 1/2060 x 1/324 x 1/149 = **1/100,000,000**

Figure 9

Hardy-Weinberg equilibrium assumes that allele frequencies will remain constant within a population from generation to generation as long as mating remains random. Random mating does not mean promiscuous mating. It simply means that the frequency of people with a particular genetic type mate is determined solely by the frequency of these people in the population. Therefore, if only one of the women in a population of forty women have red hair and only one man out of a population of forty men have red hair, the chances of that red headed woman and that red headed man randomly mating is 1/40 x 1/40 or 1 in 1600. This is the product rule which underlies random mating. The Hardy-Weinberg principle is expressed algebraically as $P^2+2pq+Q^2=1$, where p and q are different alleles. Where, for example, p and q are Rh positive and Rh negative

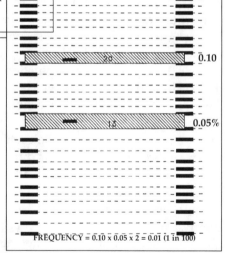

Figure 9(a)

blood types respectively and where Rh positive blood is seen is 60% of the population and Rh negative blood is seen in 40% of the population, the equation tells us that $P^2 = .36$, $2pq = .48$, and $Q^2 =.16$. Since these numbers total 1, the population is in Hardy-Weinberg equilibrium for these alleles.

Genetic Fingerprinting:

To determine the frequency with which a given allele observed on an individual's DNA occurs in a population which is in equilibrium, the scientist consults the database. If, for example, a given allele occurs in 10% of the database, there is a 1 in 10 chance that two DNA samples which show this allele come from the same individual. If the allele occurs in .01% of the database, the chance of a match is 1 in 1,000 and so forth. Where three or four rare alleles occur in a single DNA sample, the frequency with which each occurs is multiplied by the frequency of occurrences of the others. The result can be a large number, say 1 in 10 billion. Since there are less than 6 billion humans on this planet, if this is the conclusion reached by the population geneticist, the likelihood that the DNA samples came from the same individual is all but certainly established (the only uncertainty arises from the fact that the DNA of every person on the planet has not been tested, and thus there remains the slight chance that someone out there might match the forensic sample. However, keep in mind, that not everyone's fingerprints are on file either.) It is for this reason that DNA identification technology can be of enormous value for forensic purposes [*See Figure 9; Figure 9(a)demonstrates binning*].

Most, if not all, of the current scientific controversy regarding the forensic use of DNA typing technology centers on questions pertaining to the scientific validity of the current databases and to the defining of data for purposes of population genetic analysis.

The first area of discussion, relating to the validity of the current database, concerns the extent to which population substructure within large racial classifications may affect the assumptions that the existing laboratories' current databasess are both in Hardy-Weinberg equilibrium and free from linkage disequilibrium. The second, relating to the way the data is defined, concerns appropriate binning methodology.

7(a)   The Population Substructure Controversy:

As well as involving the TWGDAM guidelines, direct and cross examination will probably focus on this topic also. Therefore some detail is required. This stuff is extremely technical. To avoid misrepresentations and pre-judgments, I have quoted liberally from the articles. I realize that the following account is difficult to understand, but you will need some detail in order to prepare yourself in understanding these areas which will undoubtedly be the subject of direct and cross examination of the experts in the courtroom. You will unquestionably notice that the population geneticists who testify for the defense advocate extremely conservative views, while the experts for the prosecution are satisfied with the methods presently in use.

Currently all laboratories define their databases in terms of broad racial classifications. Lifecodes divides its database into Black, Caucasian, and Hispanic categories, while the FBI divides its database into Black, Caucasian, Eastern Hispanic (e.g., Puerto Rican) and South Western Hispanic (e.g., Mexican) and Asian categories. After these laboratories receive a defendant's blood and test it, they then compare the results against the database that corresponds to the defendant's "race". Some highly respected population geneticists argue that these classifications are too broad to be meaningful and do not account for the fact that, while ethnic Irish and ethnic Russians are both "Caucasian", genetically they are diverse.

Following the battle of the experts at the *Frye* hearing that resulted in *U.S. v. Yee*, 134 F.R.D. 161 (N.D. Ohio 1991), Richard C. Lewontin, of Harvard, and Daniel L. Hartl, of Washington University School of Medicine (both of whom had testified for the defense) published an article in *Science* magazine, perhaps the United State's most prestigious scientific journal, entitled: *Population Genetics in Forensic DNA Typing*, 254 Science 1745 (December 20, 1991). In it they challenge the notion (underlying the Hardy-Weinberg principle) that mating in the United States is truly random. Although they acknowledge that Americans rarely choose their mates on the basis of their genetic structure, they argue that random mating, in its broad sense, means that individuals choose their mates without regard to religion, ethnicity, geography, and so on. But, they point out, human populations typically form endogamous groups are based on precisely these characteristics, and individuals tend to marry within their group.

From this foundation, they point to the undisputed fact that there are striking geographical differences across Europe with regard to the ABO blood types: the frequency of the B allele is 5-10% in Britain and Ireland, increases across Eastern Europe, and reaches 25-30% in what was then the Soviet Union; the frequency of the O allele is 70-80% in Sardinians, Irish, and Scottish populations, but lower in Eastern European populations. And the blood group frequencies in southern Spain are similar to those in the near East and North Africa, reflecting six centuries of Arab rule in the southern Iberian peninsula. Although the last Muslim kingdom was expelled from Spain in 1492, the genetic legacy lingers after 500 years. The blood group Le9(a-b-) has frequencies of 3.8% in Scots, 28.7% in Swedes, and 32.4 % in Greeks; Kell (+) varies from 3% in Italians to 11% in Poles; and Lu(a+) varies from 0.86% in Welsh to 8.5% in Irish to 10% in Poles.

On the basis of this and other data, they conclude that, for these genes, there is, on average, one-third more genetic variation among Irish, Spanish, Italians, Slavs, Swedes, and other subpopulations, than there is, on the average, between Europeans, Asians, Africans, Amerinds, and Oceanians.

How do these facts skew the FBI's database? Lewontin and Hartl argue that, in terms of actual numbers of people, most immigration from Europe occurred relatively recently, and that most adult Caucasians are the grand-children of immigrants. They believe that while the notion of an American "melting pot" is true for some aspects of culture, it is not true for marriages which are strongly affected by religion and ethnicity. As a result, they con-clude, there has been insufficient time for random mixing of genes from diverse populations of origin. The consequences are twofold. First, there exists no single homogenous reference group to which all individuals can be referred for estimating probabilities of a random match of DNA type. Rather each particular individual may require a specialized grouping com-posed of appropriate ethnic or geographic subpopulations. Second, if sub-populations differ in their allele frequencies at two different loci, then these loci will not be in linkage equilibrium in the population as a whole. (That is, if a Swede marries a Swede, there is a greater likelihood that the offspring will have Le(a-b-) blood than if the Swede married a Scot. Thus in the Swede/Swede children there is an unacceptable risk that other genes, for instance the VNTR under examination, will be linked to the blood gene and will not have passed randomly to the offspring). If this is so, then a data-base that contains these alleles is not in linkage equilibrium, and the multi-plication rule across multiple VNTR loci does not apply.

Also, bins[52] that are well represented in one population sample but near-ly absent in another are a frequent occurrence among loci with large numbers of alleles. In this case, the use of the wrong ethnic group as a reference popu-lation can cause severe problems, for a VNTR type that is actually quite preva-lent in a particular subpopulation might be read as being extremely rare. The result is that a probability estimate of one in several billion is generated by the laboratory when in fact that actual frequency is one in a thousand.

To correct this problem, Lewontin and Hartl advocate a cessation of the use of the multiplication rule until a thorough and complete genetic sample of each population subgroup has been investigated.

In the same issue of *Science*, Ranajit Chakraborty, of the University of Texas, and Kenneth Kidd, of Yale, (who testified for the prosecution in the *Yee* case) published a rejoinder entitled: *The Utility of DNA Typing in Forensic Work*, 254 *Science* 1735 (December 20, 1991). They argue that the VNTR loci used by U.S. crime labs (D1S7, D2S44, D4S139, D10S28, and D17S79)[53] were chosen on the basis of their power to discriminate between genotypes observed in different individuals, and that they perform this function well within the existing databases. Then, in a highly technical assault on Lewontin and Hartl's data—the dint of which is that their blood group figures are out of date—they purport to demonstrate that the dire predictions about the effect of Caucasian subpopulation on the databases is unfounded.

For the judge, lawyer and layman, the most intelligible portion of the article concerns their rebuttal to Lewontin and Hartl's argument concerning our marriage patterns as it affects population genetics. They note, as do Lewontin and Hartl, that regardless of what else might prompt the decision to marry another, that decision is truly random with respect to VNTRs and blood types. They also assail the generalizations regarding American marriage practice studies done before the "baby boom", on which Lewontin and Hartl rely in part, because such studies do not reflect the extensive mobility and mixing of groups in the general U.S. population that occurred following World War II. They assert that,

> "The present generation of Americans, the group most likely to commit violent crimes, are offspring of this postwar era, which is also an era in which multiple marriages are more frequent. In summary, American demography for descendants of Caucasian immigrants is closer to a 'melting pot' than to a rigid subdivision...Thus, we are not concerned with estimating the frequency of a DNA profile among individuals who have the same ethnic ancestry as a defendant, for example, one-eighth Irish, one-fourth Italian, one-eighth French, and one-fourth Amerindian; no such database will ever exist, nor is it necessary. In this example, the U.S. Caucasian database and the U.S. Hispanic database from the Southwest provide conservative estimates that indicate the degree of uncertainty that might exist... it is the general frequency in the total population that is desired, not the frequency in the subgroup to which the suspect or defendant belongs."

In the February 7, 1992 edition of *Science*, Neil J. Risch and B. Devlin (both of the Division of Biostatistics at Yale) joined the fray in an article entitled: *On the Probability of Matching DNA Fingerprints*, 255 *Science* 717. In it they begin with the familiar principle that, for the multiplication rule to be valid, the genetic events recorded in the database must be statistically independent, and that this includes both statistical independence within a locus (i.e., Hardy-Weinberg equilibrium), and statistical independence across loci (i.e., linkage equilibrium). They posit the hypothesis that: "If population substructure were a serious problem, leading to significant departures from statistical independence, certain VNTR genotype patterns might occur significantly more often than independence would predict, and hence the probability that two unrelated individuals, having a matching DNA pattern, could be considerably higher than usually reported." (at p. 718).

Then they tested both the FBI and the Lifecodes databases to determine whether there is statistical independence of genotypes matching across sets of loci (linkage equilibrium) and to determine the probability that two random, unrelated individuals have matching genotypes at more than one VNTR loci. The FBI database was tested at D1S7, D2S44, D4S139, D10S7, and D17S79, and the Lifecodes database was tested at D2S44, D14S13, and D17S79.

Separate tests are required because, although both laboratories analyze two of the same loci (D2S44 and D17S79), they use different restriction enzymes. The FBI uses HAE III which results in smaller fragments than those generated by Lifecodes which, at that time, used PST 1. The longer fragments result in higher match probabilities.[54]

After examining both databases for Caucasians, Blacks, and Hispanics, Risch and Devlin found that Blacks have the lowest match probabilities for all loci, reflecting the fact that the Black population has the greatest gene diversity. Caucasians and Hispanics have similar match probabilities. In the FBI database there was one, three-locus match between a Caucasian and a Southeast Hispanic (at D2S44, D4S139, and D17S79) out of 7,628,360 total comparisons for all ethnic groups combined. There were no four locus matches.

For Lifecodes, with the loci taken as pairs, there were a total of 9,674,639 comparisons between ethnic groups and 11,230 matches observed, for an overall rate of 0.00116.

Thus, according to Risch and Devlin, "The observed independence of matching among loci, both in the FBI and Lifecodes data sets, provides no support for claims of linkage disequilibrium within ethnic groups. Indeed, if linkage disequilibrium among loci does exist, it has little effect on the probability of two random individuals having matching genotypes" (at p. 719). For a random match across five loci, "...the most common five-locus genotype can be no more frequent than 1 in 4,230,000 in Blacks, 1 in 1,090,000 in Caucasians, 1 in 1,310,000 in Southeast Hispanics, and 1 in 870,000 in Southwest Hispanics. Therefore, although matching five-locus genotype patterns may exist (that is, everyone is not automatically unique), the number of such matches is vanishingly small compared to the population size....Although we find the probability of a matching DNA profile between unrelated individuals to be vanishingly small, especially at five loci, related individuals, in particular identical twins and siblings, have a far greater probability of matching genotypes. For identical twins, the probability is 1.0 while for siblings it is 0.001. Therefore, in the forensic setting, we conclude that an innocent suspect has little to fear from DNA evidence, unless he or she has an evil twin" (at p. 720).

The controversy continued in the letters to the editor section of the

February 28, 1992 edition of *Science*, 255 *Science* 1051-55. Five letters from scientists around the country appeared along with responses from Lewontin and Hartl and Chakraborty and Kidd. This controversy will continue unabated until databases contain data from every ethnic type to provide an authoritative answer. This much is clear: VNTRs do not behave like other, more well documented areas of the genome, like bloodtypes.

Thus there is lots of room for argument, and in some states, which follow the *Frye* standard for the admission of new scientific evidence, the substructure controversy has sufficed to preclude admission of DNA evidence.[55]

7(b) The Ceiling Principle:

The ceiling method for population genetics calculation was recommended by the April, 1992 report of the National Academy of Sciences Committee on DNA Technology in Forensic Science as a practical and sound approach for accounting for error based on possible population substructure. It proceeds upon the assumption that the multiplication rule will yield conservative (i.e., pro-defendant) estimates, even for a substructured population, provided that the allele frequencies used in the multiplication calculation exceed the allele frequencies in any of the population subgroups.

How is this to be done? The committee advocates taking random samples from 100 persons in each of 15-20 targeted subpopulations which are relatively homogenous genetically, and taking the largest frequency in any of these populations or five percent, whichever is larger, as the ceiling frequency. The committee uses the following illustrations:

"Suppose that two loci have been studied in three population samples with the following results:

	Population 1	Population 2	Population 3
Locus 1			
Allele a	1%	5%	11%
Allele b	5%	8%	10%
Locus 2			
Allele c	3%	4%	4%
Allele d	2%	15%	7%

For the genotype consisting of a/b at locus 1 and c/d at locus 2, the ceiling principle would assign ceiling values of 11% for allele a, 10% for allele b, 5% for allele c, and 15% for allele d and would apply the multiplication rule to yield a genotype frequency of $[2(0.11)(0.10)][2(0.5)(0.15)] = 0.00033$, or about 1 in 3,000.

Genetic Fingerprinting:

Note that the frequency used for allele c is 5% rather than 4%, to reflect the recommended lower bound for each allele frequency."

Any lack of discriminating power caused by this very conservative approach to the multiplication rule can be remedied by employing additional probes.[56]

7(c) Bins, and Binning Procedures:

A "bin" is an arbitrarily defined area of the genome, i.e., one lab may pick that portion that, say, lies between 750 KB and 1123 KB as bin #1 and that portion between 11,782 KB and 11,989 KB as bin #2. Actually the selection of a bin size is not quite that arbitrary; it is based upon the scientist's statistical analysis of the database and the scientist's judgment as to which bin sizes will be most informative for estimating the frequency with which alleles are found across the entire spectrum of the genome. But the point to be made is that there is no scientifically demonstrable requirement for defining a bin in a particular way; the decision is left to the individual laboratory, and one laboratory's bins do not have to be compatible with those of another laboratory. *[See Figure 9(a) page 78.]*

The arbitrary nature of the binning process has led to past abuses of the technology. For example, before the *Castro* case was litigated, Lifecodes used a wide margin of inclusion when it determined that two bands matched on the autorad, but with a very small margin of inclusion when it defined its bins for purposes of population genetics.[57] For example, two bands falling anywhere between 100 KB and 500 KB could be called a match at 250 KB, but for purposes of population genetics, the relevant bin would be defined as falling between 240 KB and 260 KB. The result of this practice was that the reported figures for the probability of a person other than the suspect matching the forensic sample, became astronomic. In one case, based on a total database of only 500 individuals, a laboratory calculated a match probability of 1 in 738 trillion (based on four loci) and 1 in 450 million (based on two loci). Obviously, these numbers are very impressive to a jury, but in fact they are the product of bad science. In order to convey accurate numbers, the "window" for declaring a match on the autorad must be no larger than the "window" of the bin into which they are sized. (See Figure 6.) Lifecodes now uses the same window for its match declaration and its bins. However, the debate over proper binning methods will continue. Presently, the binning method chosen by the FBI appears to be gaining favor in the courts.

7(d) FBI Binning Methodology: (See *U.S. v. Yee*, 134 F.R.D. 161 [N.D. Ohio 1991] for an excellent analysis of the issues)

In *Yee*, to reach its estimate of the likelihood of a non-random match, 1 in 35,000, the FBI used a fixed bin method, with a statistical safety measure of collapsing into each other, bins that contain fewer than five occurrences. Thus, if a particular bin displays fewer than five occurrences, it is merged into the adjacent bin and this process is continued until there is a total of at least five bands in each bin. If a band lies at the border of two bins, it is assigned to the bin containing the largest number of occurrences, and because the FBI uses a plus-or-minus 2.5% measurement window, a forensic band is said to fall on the border of a bin where any portion of the possible range of sizes for the band are those that are within that window and fall on a bin border. In *Yee*, the court rejected a challenge to the FBI's Caucasian database based on variations in the blood types among various European Caucasian nationalities and leading to the inference that the same must hold true for the VNTRs used in forensic analysis, i.e., "substructure" (The Lewontin/Hartl position). The court found that the FBI adequately compensates for substructure (if, in fact, it exists for these alleles) by:

(1) its fixed bin structure which overstates the true frequency of any allele
(2) use of bins that are wider than the match window
(3) clustering alleles when fewer than five are present in a given bin
(4) allocation of borderline bins to the bin with the larger frequency
(5) use of the 2P factor (i.e., two times P rather than P squared) when a single band is encountered

Objections to the FBI's methodology were determined to go to the weight rather than the admissibility of the estimate of allele frequency [*See Figure 8, supra*].

As of June, 1995, the FBI binning methodology resulted in the collapse of 31 possible bins into 24 bins as this permitted as least five occurrences within each bin, pursuant to their current database. The FBI appears to use very conservative procedures to generate their population estimates. The FBI uses a conservative formula because they cannot be sure that a sir.gle band which appears on their gel is in fact a homozygous band unless they have the DNA of both parents of the person whose DNA is being examined. Nonetheless, the FBI reported the likelihood of a match as 1 in 6 million for Caucasians, 1 in 11 million for Blacks and 1 in 9 million for Hispanics in a July, 1995 murder case during a hearing in Bronx County, where there was a four probe match. Under the ceiling principle, the figure was reduced to 1 in 161,000. People v. *Gregory Watson*, Supreme Court, Bronx County, September 11, 1995. (Not officially reported). See also, *United States* v. *Bonds, infra*.

SUMMARY OF "DNA TECHNOLOGY IN FORENSIC SCIENCE"

"[as] DNA typing entered the courtrooms of this country, questions appeared about its reliability and methodological standards and about the interpretation of population statistics.

By the summer of 1989, a crescendo of questions concerning DNA typing had been raised in connection with some well-publicized criminal cases, and calls for the examination of the issues by the National Research Council of the National Academy of Sciences came from the scientific and legal communities." (Pg. vii)

Because several courts in various jurisdictions have placed great emphasis on the report issued by the National Research Council, herewith is a summary of that 1992 document. *(Page numbers of the report are in parenthesis.)*

I SUMMARY

A. A "Match" without valid estimate of frequency is meaningless. (9)

B. The Committee *assumes* the existence of population substructuring and recommends estimation method for four reasons:

1. Conservative estimates do not emasculate inherent power of DNA typing

2. Conservative estimates can be countered by typing at additional loci

3. General approach will be applicable to additional loci as discovered

4. Desirable to develop method independent of ethnic group of subject (12-13)

C. Recommends use of the "ceiling principle":

1. Ceiling frequency for each allele at each locus, representing

upper bound and independent of ethnic background of subject

2. Application of multiplication rule (product rule) for calculation of genotype frequency, using ceiling allele frequencies (13)

D. Determination of ceiling frequencies:

1. Drawing of random samples of 100 persons from each of 15-20 populations, representing "largely" genetically homogeneous groups
2. Utilize as ceiling frequency the actual allelic frequency or 5%, whichever is larger

3. Ignore ethnic background of subject (14-15)

E. "That no evidence of population substructure is demonstrable with the markers tested so far cannot be taken to mean that such does not exist for other markers" (13-14)

F. Method for use in interval regarding matches until population studies completed:

1. Comparison to population databank and fact no match within "n", consisting of number of profiles in database

2. 95% confidence interval calculated for each allele, with highest allelic frequency used, or 10%, whichever is higher, among at least three major "races" (e.g., Caucasians, Blacks, Hispanics, Asians)

3. Multiplication of above frequencies (14-15)

G. Standardization of laboratory procedures required to ensure high quality results for court (15):

1. Each laboratory must have formal, detailed quality assurance ("QA") and quality control ("QC") programs

2. FBI "TWGDAM" ("Technical Working Group on DNA Analysis and Methods) program excellent starting point

3. Potential mechanisms are individual certification, laboratory accreditation and state or federal regulation

4. Courts should require that DNA labs providing evidence be properly accredited for each typing method used, or demonstrate that meet same standards as accredited laboratories (16-17)

H. DNA databanks of felons convicted of certain crimes should be created in the future, likely using new technologies, if pilot studies demonstrate utility (19)

I. Courts should take judicial notice of following:

1. DNA study, in principle, is reliable method to compare samples

2. DNA of each person, except identical twins, is unique

3. RFLP analysis, using single-locus probes, is "fundamentally sound," although particular use depends on reproducibility and use of proper controls

4. Admissibility of evidence should be adjudicated on case-by-case basis, including issues of accreditation, certification, etc. (23)

II INTRODUCTION

Any forensic DNA method, as with medical DNA and other testing, "should be rapid, accurate, and inexpensive" (48)

III TECHNICAL CONSIDERATIONS

A. New DNA typing methods or "substantial variation" of existing technique requires publication and scientific scrutiny (56)

B. Band shifting:

1. Recommend testing of all samples for band shifting by use of monomorphic probes covering wide range of fragment sizes in gels (60)

2. Recommend further study of "band shifting"—until such studies completed and published, samples showing apparent shifting should be declared inconclusive (61)

C. Match criteria must be utilized such that patterns outside be declared inconclusive or nonmatching (61) [*See Figure 9 and 9(a)*]

D. Polymerase Chain Reaction ("PCR"):

   1. Technical considerations

      a. Precise conditions must be established for each system and must be "thoroughly characterized" for sensitivity (64)
      b. Unstained controls must be utilized for interpretation assistance (66)
      c. Contamination risks can be reduced by careful procedures (66-67)

   2. Prospects of PCR-based methods

      a. "It is well-established that one can greatly amplify a locus with authenticity and that one can reliably detect alleles or sequence variation at the amplified locus with any of a number of techniques" (70)
      b. "The theory of PCR analysis, even though it is the analysis of synthetic DNA, as opposed to the natural sample, is scientifically accepted and has been accepted by a number of courts" (70)
      c. Settled that DQ-Alpha locus following PCR amplification can "provide useful information during the investigative phase in the forensic setting" (70)

E. National Committee on Forensic DNA Typing should be created to provide advice on scientific and technical issues as they occur (71)

IV STATISTICAL INTERPRETATION

A. Match between two DNA patterns using 3-5 loci "can be considered strong evidence" that the samples are from a common source (74)

B. A "Match," without statistical interpretation of significance, is meaningless (74)

Genetic Fingerprinting:

C. Independence and multiplication rule (product rule):

1. Insufficient body of data to claim frequency calculations are valid per se (77)

2. Assumption of independence must "be strictly scrutinized and estmate procedures appropriately adjusted" (77)

3. Analysis of FBI database resulted in no five-locus matches; closest match was one, three-locus match from 7.6 million base pair comparisons (77)

4. Disagreement:

    a. Some population geneticists "believe that the absence of substructure cannot be assumed, but must be proved empirically" (80)

    b. Others, "while recognizing the possibility or likelihood of population substructure, conclude the evidence to date suggests that the effect on estimates of genotype frequencies are minimal"(80)

    c. Empirical data studied demonstrates "no deviation from independence within or across loci" (Weir) (80)

5. Committee "chosen to assume for the sake of discussion that population substructure may exist and provide a method for estimating population frequencies in a manner that adequately accounts for it" (80):

    a. Inherent power of DNA typing not invaded by conservative estimation process
    b. Lost statistical power can be countered by examination of additional loci
    c. General approach can be applied to any loci ultimately used in typing
    d. Frequency estimation can be used without reference to ethnic group of subject (80)

D. Sub Group sampling:
   1. Proper way to detect genetic variation in subgroups is to directly sample and analyze (81)

   2. Hardy-Weinberg Equilibrium test is "very weak" for determining substructure (82)

   3. Studies "have shown that the genetic diversity between subgroups within races is greater than the genetic variation between races" (82)

E. Ceiling principle (see "Summary," above):

   1. Determination of ceiling frequency for each allele, utilizing upper confidence level, independent of ethnic origin of subject, followed by genotype frequency applying product rule (83-85)

   2. Random sampling and testing of 100 persons from each of 15-20 largely homogeneous populations; largest frequency at each allele, or 5%, whichever larger, shall be ceiling frequency (83)

   3. Ethnic background of subject to be ignored (85)

   4. "Although the ceiling principle is a conservative approach, we feel that it is appropriate, because DNA typing is unique in that the forensic analyst has an essentially unlimited ability to adduce additional evidence. Whatever power is sacrificed by requiring conservative estimates can be regained by examining additional loci" (85)

F. Laboratory error rates must be estimated on regular basis through use of blind proficiency testing and revealed to juries (89)

G. Interim statistical frequency calculation (see "Summary," above):

   1. Comparison of patterns to existing laboratory database and reporting of "n"

   2. Calculation of frequency based on use of ceiling frequency with at least three major groups, assuming that Hardy-Weinberg and linkage equilibrium studies are verified for loci

utilized with proper band measurement methods:

a. 95% confidence for each allele, using largest
   frequency or 10%, whichever is larger
b. Application of multiplication rule
c. Notes that frequency calculation is "a reasonable
   scientific judgment based on available data" and
   assumption about U.S. populations that is still under
   examination (91- 92)

H. If completion of 15-20 population groups verifies absence of significant substructure, 5% lower bound may be used at that point (93)

I. "We emphasize that our recommendations are not intended to question previous cases, but rather to chart the most prudent course for
the future" (93)

J. Population databases must be available for "reasonable scientific
inspection" (93-94)

V ENSURING HIGH STANDARDS

A. Standardization necessary to ensure high-quality results (98)

B. Formal, detailed QA programs necessary; TWGDAM guidelines
recommended to be used formally (99)

C. Regulation

1. "Courts should require that a proponent of DNA typing
   evidence have appropriate accreditation—including
   demonstration of external, blind proficiency testing (as
   well as other accreditation that might be mandated by
   government or come to be generally accepted in the pro-
   fession)—for its evidence to be admissible" (106-107)

2. Meanwhile, should require DNA laboratory to show
   that "effectively" following accreditation requirements
   of TWG DAM and this report (107)

3. Federal legislation should be adopted to require

accreditation of all laboratories performing DNA typing (107)

4. "Courts should require that proponents of DNA typing evidence have proper accreditation for each DNA typing method used. Lack of accreditation should be considered a prima facie case that a laboratory has not complied with generally accepted standards" (109)

VI FORENSIC DNA DATABANKS AND PRIVACY OF INFORMATION

A. "The committee believes that it is too early to launch a comprehensive national DNA profile databank" (116)

B. Information should only be accessible to and utilized by authorized persons (128)

C. Existing RFLP technology unlikely to represent wise technique for databanking due to development of newer methods (129)

D. Databanking "match" should only be used for purposes of probable cause to obtain further samples and further testing using markers at additional loci (129)

VII USE OF DNA IN THE LEGAL SYSTEM

A. Judicial Notice

1. Appropriate for court to judicially notice that except for identical twins, each person's DNA is different

2. Appropriate for court to judicially notice that RFLP analysis valid procedure for use with blood, semen, and other materials, although "additional questions of reliability are raised" with respect to application in forensic science

3. Proper procedure is to evaluate these concerns on case-by-case basis as opposed to generally excluding DNA evidence; particularly important is demonstration laboratory accredited and personnel certified (133-134)

4. Adequacy of statistical databanks unproven, such that conservative estimation procedures, as described above, should be utilized (134)

5. Proper analysis in given case must be resolved prior to admissibility; evidence should not be admissible unless proper procedures followed; "the probative force of the evidence will depend on the quality of the laboratory work" (134)

B. Hearings on new technology or variations

1. No longer any question regarding fact DNA can be used to obtain identification information (144)

2. New probe, e.g., in RFLP analysis may require admissibility hearing (144)

3. Court can limit inquiry to "substantially novel aspects of the technology, focusing on whether the method is accepted for scientific applications and whether it has been validated for forensic identification" (144-145)

C. Hearings on existing technology:

"In view of the importance of DNA typing in both civil and criminal cases, the judge should determine, before allowing DNA evidence to be introduced, that appropriate standards have been followed, that tests were adequately performed by a reliable laboratory, and that the appropriate protocols for DNA typing and formulation of an opinion were fully complied with" (145)

1. Extensive admissibility hearings no longer necessary regarding general validity, although questions about procedures to report a match "will be questioned" in some cases (145)

2. Conservative approach should be employed regarding assumptions about use of product rule; "a considerable degree of discretion and control by the courts in these cases is recommended" (145)

3. "Ultimately, DNA typing evidence should be used without any greater inconvenience than traditional fingerprint evidence" (146)

D. Roles of criminal justice system participants:

1. Prosecution responsibility to fully reveal to defense counsel and defense experts all information to enable evidence evaluation, including information about tests performed (146)

2. Sample portions for retesting by independent analysts should be preserved when possible

3. "DNA evidence, like other scientific and statistical evidence, can pose special problems of jury comprehension. Courts and attorneys should cooperate to facilitate jury understanding. Innovative techniques, such as allowing jurors to take notes or ask questions, might be considered. Jargon should be avoided, and information should be presented simply, clearly, and fairly. Unless limited by law or court rules, judges should be free to pose questions to witnesses when they feel that the answers might clarify the testimony. Reports and relevant materials should be admitted into evidence so that they can be studied by courts at their leisure. Finally, a judge would not be amiss in pointing out to attorneys the wisdom of including jurors who are found to have a background that enhances their ability to understand the expert testimony" (147)

4. Reservations about errors or deficiencies should be revealed by testing laboratories. Failure to do so should be dealt with seriously, including the use of contempt and/or exclusion of testimony by experts who "have misled deliberately in the past" (148)

E. "The quality of justice will be increased by full use of DNA typing" (149)

VIII DNA TYPING AND SOCIETY

A. "DNA identification is not only a way of securing convictions; it is also a way of excluding suspects who might otherwise be falsely charged with and convicted of serious crimes" (156)

Genetic Fingerprinting:

B. Considering current technology and databases, "a witness or prosecutor will seldom (if ever) be justified in stating that the probability that a reported DNA match involves someone other than the suspect is so low as to make that possibility entirely implausible" (161)

C. Presentations to judges or juries that DNA typing is infallible should rarely be made. See examples used (161)

SECTION I

A COMPARISON OF RFLP & PCR

RFLP

1. High quality DNA and not degraded
2. Need 50+ nanograms (dime size)
3. Very discriminating
4. 6-8 weeks to complete

PCR

1. DNA can be degraded
2. Need 10+ nanograms
3. Not as powerful; numbers are much less
4. Polymarker PCR will increase power and numbers
5. 1-2 weeks to complete

TYPES OF EVIDENCE USED

1. Vaginal swabs
2. Semen stains
3. Bloodstains (dime size)
4. Seeds from tree clippings

1. Cigarette butts
2. Pipes
3. Pens
4. Envelopes
5. Stamps
6. Phones
7. Fingernails
8. Fecal matter
9. Vomit
10. Nasal mucous (tissue)
11. Vaginal slides
12. Blood splatters
13. Old stains

PROBES GENERALLY USED IN RFLP:

* 1. D1S7   (1st chromosome; 7th location)
* 2. D2S44   (2nd chromosome; 44th location)
* 3. D4S139 (4th chromosome; 139th location)
  4. D4S163 (4th chromosome; 163rd location)
* 5. D5S110 (5th chromosome; 110th location)
  6. D10S7   (10th chromosome; 7th location)
* 7. D10S28 (10th chromosome; 28th location)
* 8. D14S13 (14th chromosome; 13th location)
* 9. D17S79 (17th chromosome; 79th location)
* 10. D18S27 (18th chromosome; 27th location)
* 11. DXYS14 (X & Y chromosome; 14th location)

* 12. DYZ1   (Y chromosome; 1st location)

* Note: Most commonly used probes in the United States.

PCR METHODS

A. DQ Alpha (242 base pairs and 6 alleles; 21 types)
   (Difference in sequence—not length; 6th Chromosome and
   inspects the gene sequence; non-polymorphic area)

B. Polymarker System. (These are genes—not polymorphic)
   1. LDLR—2 alleles—3 types (Low Density Lipoprotein Receptor—
      214bp 19th chromosome)
   2. GYPA—2 allele—3 types (Glycophorin A—190 bp
      4th chromosome)
   3. HBGG—3 alleles—6 types (Hemoglobin G Gammaglobin—172bp
      11th chromosome)
   4. GC —3 alleles—6 types (Group Specific Components-138bp
      4th chromosome)
C. AMPFLP (Amplified Fragment Length Polymorphism) PCR + RFLP
   1. D7S8— 2 alleles—3 types (7th Chromosome; 8th location)
   2. D17Z1— (17th chromosome)
   3. D1S80— (1st Chromosome; 80th location)

D. Mitochondrial DNA

E. STR (Short Tandem Repeats) on the APO-B and HUM-THOI Loci.

F. MVR (Minisatellite Variant Repeat) Examins Actual Differences in
Base Pair Sequences.

The six forms (alleles) of DQ Alpha are: 1.1, 1.2, 1.3, 2, 3, 4.
The twenty one different possible combinations of the six alleles are as follows:

1. 1.1, 1.1
2. 1.1, 1.2
3. 1.1, 1.3
4. 1.1, 2
5. 1.1, 3
6. 1.1, 4
7. 1.2, 1.2
8. 1.2, 1.3
9. 1.2, 2
10. 2, 3
11. 1.2, 4
12. 1.3, 1.3
13. 1.3, 2
14. 1.3, 3
15. 1.3, 4
16. 2, 2
17. 2, 3
18. 2, 4
19. 3, 3
20. 3, 4
21. 4, 4

Ex: 1.1 from father and 1.1 from mother = 1.1, 1.1

1.1 from father and 1.3 from mother = 1.1, 1.3.

One lab, using DQ Alpha and LDLR, GYPA, HBGG, GC and D7S8, generated population frequencies as follows:

1 in 906,000 Caucasians;

1 in 11,819 African Americans;

1 in 630,700 Hispanics.

A person may be included in PCR DQ-Alpha, but excluded by RFLP or Polymarker, because these tests are much more discriminating.

§ 1 ALABAMA:

In *Ex parte Perry v. Alabama*, 586 So.2d 242 (Ala. Sup. Ct. 1991) [*on remand* 586 So.2d 256 (Ct. of Crim. App. 1991)], a Lifecodes generated RFLP test was ruled to be inadmissible on the basis of trial testimony alone[58] under a *Frye* standard which adopts the three-prong test set forth in *People v. Castro, infra*. However, the third prong was modified to state:

> "In this particular case, did the testing
> laboratory perform generally accepted scientific
> techniques without error in the performance or
> interpretation of the tests. We believe that our
> statement of the third prong says in substance what
> the court in *Castro* meant" (586 So.2d at 250).

The testimony given by Lifecodes' employees that procedures used were generally accepted, was found to be insufficient to support that assertion. Therefore the court concluded that the record was insufficient to determine whether there was error in the performance and interpretation of the test. The court also rejected the statistical estimate of a random match of 1 in 209 million under the three-prong *Castro* standard on the grounds that the expert testimony was too limited and too conclusory to support its admission.

The court noted that it shared the same concerns as expressed in *Minnesota v. Schwartz*, 447 N.W.2d 442 (Minn. Sup. Ct. 1989) (discussed infra at J§21) in that large numbers create "a potentially exaggerated impact on the trier of fact", and held that even if the estimate is admissible as a matter of science, it may nonetheless be excluded if its prejudicial impact outweighs its probative value (586 So.2d at 254). The court required an admissibility hearing outside the jury's presence in future cases and remanded the *Perry* cases for a hearing to determine the admissibility of the DNA evidence.

Following that hearing, the intermediate appellate court found that Lifecodes' estimate of 1 in 209 million was the result of a clerical error in juxtaposing two fragment sizes. It found that Lifecodes' new estimate of 1 in 12 billion (based on, *inter alia*, two new hybridizations performed after the trial in this case) was reliable, and it noted that even defendant's expert calculated the estimate to be 1 in 300 million at the lowest. Accordingly, the court affirmed the conviction noting that any error was harmless. *Perry v.*

Alabama, 606 So.2d 224 (Ala. Ct. Crim. App. 1992). See also *Snowden v. Alabama*, 574 So.2d 960 (Ala. Ct. Crim. App. 1990). See *Alabama v. Hutcherson*, No. CR-92-925, 1994 WL 228861 (Ala. Crim. App. May 27, 1994) (The Court held that DNA testing is generally accepted in the scientific community. However, in this case, insufficient evidence was presented demonstrating reliability of the test required by the three-pronged test as set forth by the Alabama Supreme Court in *Ex parte Perry*); *Seritt v. Alabama*, 647 So.2d 1 (Ala. Crim. App. 1994). See also, *Alabama v. DuBose*, 1995 WL 124653 (Ala. Sup. Ct. 3/24/95) (*Rev'd.*; Defendant entitled to assigned DNA expert). In *Payne v. Alabama*, 1995 WL 316918 (Ala. Ct. Crim. App.) decided May 26, 1995, the court affirmed the murder conviction of the defendant and a sentence of death. The court noted that the defendant failed to request a pretrial hearing outside the presence of the jury nor did he object to the admission of PCR DQ-Alpha testing at trial. No hearing need be held unless the DNA evidence is challenged and the defendant requests a pretrial hearing outside the presence of the jury. Accord, *Meyers v. Alabama*, 1995 WL 664621 (Ala. Ct. Crim. App) November 9, 1995.

§ 2 ARIZONA:

The facts in *Arizona v. Bible*, 858 P.2d 1152 (Ariz. Sup. Ct. 1993), demonstrate the corroborative nature of DNA evidence and its place alongside other overwhelming circumstantial evidence. This case also illustrates the struggle courts encounter when dealing with statistical probabilities.

The defendant was charged with the murder and rape of a nine year old girl. The family of the deceased saw her riding her bicycle just prior to her disappearance. They also noticed and reported a van being driven by a man who, when passing them on the road, looked at them strangely. The child's bike was discovered abandoned a short distance from this encounter.

In an unrelated dispute, the brother of the defendant reported a theft by the defendant. The description of the defendant and his van offered by the brother matched the description previously supplied by the victim's mother. Further police investigation revealed that the van was stolen from the police pound and had damage to the left rear panel. The defendant was arrested when police observed him in the van which had been freshly painted a different color. The defendant admitted stealing the van and re-painting it, but denied any knowledge of the still missing youngster or her location. The van had been used for newspaper deliveries and had a large quantity of rubber bands in the rear. Police noticed that a case of "Suntory Vodka" in the van had two bottles missing. Also noted was a "Dutchmaster" cigar along with its wrapper and band in the ashtray. Also in the van were

"Carnation Rich" hot chocolate packets. A piece of metal from the damaged portion of the van was in the trunk along with a green blanket. Finally, the police observed some blood. The defendant was wearing a blood splattered shirt which had tobacco residue in the pocket.

Three weeks later, the youngster's body, wrapped in a sheet, was discovered in a field. Found in the area of the body were "Dutchmaster" cigars which were forensically determined to be extremely similar to the cigar found in the van and the tobacco residue in the defendant's shirt pocket.

Also near the body was an empty ten pack of "Carnation Rich" hot chocolate packets.

A further search discovered two empty "Suntory Vodka" bottles which were in all respects identical to the bottles found in the van.

Surrounding the child's body were numerous rubber bands which were forensically determined to be exactly identical to the rubber bands found in the van.

Pieces of metal found near the body exactly fit the damaged portion of the van and another piece of metal previously retrieved from the van.

Hair retrieved from the defendant's shirt was found to be similar to the child's hair. Hair of the youngster was also found in the van and on a blanket in the van. Hair similar to the defendant's was found on the sheet covering the body and on the victim's t-shirt. A lock of the victim's hair pulled from her head and found near the body also contained a pubic hair determined to be similar to the defendant's.

Fibers found in this lock of hair were determined to be similar to the lining of the jacket the defendant was wearing when arrested. Fibers found near the body were forensically determined to be from van's seat cover. Also, additional fibers found at the scene and on the shoelaces used to tie the hands of the nine year old victim were identified as coming from the defendant's jacket lining. Other fibers recovered at the scene were connected to the green blanket found in the van.

DNA testing of the blood found on the defendant's shirt was compared to the youngster's DNA and found to be a match with calculations of 1 in 14 billion, using the product rule and 1 in 60 million using a more conservative calculation.

The court concluded that a Cellmark generated RFLP test would be admissible under a *Frye* standard but its product rule calculation is not. That court noted:

> "To summarize, we hold that the principles and theory underlying DNA testing and Cellmark's match criteria are generally accepted in the relevant scientific community.

General acceptance regarding these matters permits judicial notice of DNA theory and the techniques—at least insofar as Cellmark is concerned—for ascertaining and declaring a match. From this point forward, Arizona trial courts no longer need to hold *Frye* hearings regarding the general acceptance of DNA theory, the principles underlying DNA testing, or the Cellmark match criteria. We emphasize, however, what this means and what it does not mean. If testing shows that samples do not match, then the conclusion is that they are from different individuals. If testing shows that the samples do match, the conclusion is that they may be from the same individual. We conclude that there is no general acceptance in the relevant scientific community for Cellmark's random match probability calculations. Because these calculations do not meet the *Frye* test, they are inadmissible...we hold only that statistical probability evidence based on Cellmark's database is not based on generally accepted scientific theory and is inadmissible."

Accord Arizona v. Gallegos, 870 P.2d 1097 (Ariz. Sup. Ct. 1994); *Arizona v. Clark*, 887 P.2d 572 (Ariz. Ct. App. 1994) (Court opined that admitting evidence of DNA probability calculations resulted in a high potential for unfair prejudice. Given the decision in *Bible*, the court could not conclude beyond a reasonable doubt that the erroneously admitted DNA testimony had no influence on the jury's verdict).

In *Arizona v. Hummert*, 1 CA-CR 92-098, 1994 WL 384979 (Ariz. Ct. App. July 26, 1994), the trial court admitted matching evidence but excluded statistical evidence. The appellate court reversed. The court ruled that all DNA evidence was inadmissible in the absence of generally accepted population frequency statistics.

However, in the most recent case dealing with DNA forensic evidence involving seeds and trees, the appellate court distinquished *Hummert*.

The facts in *Arizona v. Bogan*, 1995 WL 156279 (Ariz. Ct. App. 1995) revealed the following: On May 3, 1992, Tim Faulkner was riding his dirt bike. As he traveled through a dry wash in the desert near the intersection of Jack Rabbitt Trail Drive and Indian School Road, he observed the body of a nude woman, lying face down in the brush. She was lying near a cluster of Palo Verde trees. She appeared dead.

Sheriffs soon arrived and determined that she had been strangled to death. The sheriff noticed that fresh blood was on her body and concluded that her death was recent. Her clothing was scattered around the area.

Matted grass in the area led to her body. This suggested that her body had been dragged to its resting place. A cloth was tied around her neck and left wrist. A shoelace was tied around her left ankle and a braided wire was tied around her right wrist and right ankle. A vinyl strap and another braided wire were loosely lying across the victim's neck. A metal ring was attached to the braided wire. As police investigated the area, a witness informed them that he had been driving home from a party at approximately 1:30 a.m. when he noticed a vehicle exiting the area. The vehicle was a white "dually" pickup truck with amber clearing lights on the top of the cab. A "dually" is a heavy duty pick up truck with four wheels on the rear axle. The pickup was going "pretty quick."

The police, during their search, retrieved a pager just a few feet from the body. Investigation disclosed that the pager was registered to a man named Earl Bogan. His son, Alan Bogan, was the primary user of this device.

Alan Bogan also owned a white pickup truck with amber lights over the cab. It also was a "dually." Police immediately impounded the truck and conducted a thorough search. In the bed of the truck they found two seed pods from a Palo Verde tree which they seized as evidence.

Alan lived with Rebecca Franklin. She was questioned and informed the police that on May 2, 1992, a day before the murder, Alan was drinking heavily in their apartment. She left the apartment about 8:30 p.m. and when she returned at 11:30 p.m. Alan was gone. About 2:00 a.m., Alan woke her up. He had scratches on his face that had not been there earlier in the evening. He explained that he had a fight in a bar. She also told the police that Alan kept a length of braided wire in his truck which had a small metal ring attached to it. The police were unable to find the wire in the truck when they searched it.

The defendant was taken into custody and told the police that he had lied to his girlfriend. What really happened on the evening of May 2 was that he picked up a female hitchhiker. His description of her matched the deceased. He told the police that he had sexual intercourse with her in his truck. Afterward, as he was driving, they had an argument and he stopped the truck and told her to get out. She swiped his pager, his wallet and other items off the dashboard and ran away. He chased her down. They fought over his property. She scratched his face. He thought he recovered all his property, but he noticed that his pager was missing the next morning. The defendant knew the area where the deceased was discovered, but insisted that he had not been there in years. He adamantly denied killing Johnson.

Detective Charlie Norton was assigned to the homicide. He noticed that the Palo Verde tree at the crime scene had a fresh abrasion on one of its lower branches. He contacted Dr. Timothy Helentjaris, a professor of molecular genetics at the University of Arizona. Specifically, the detective asked the professor to determine if the pods came from the Palo Verde tree at the scene of the homicide. Dr. Helentjaris employed a technique known as RAPD, "Randomly Amplified Polymorphic DNA". This process allows the comparison of DNA from the seed pods with the DNA from the Palo Verde tree near the scene of the crime. The professor indicated that there are a variety of Palo Verde trees in the desert area in that county and he took samples of DNA from each of these trees. He concluded that on the basis of the DNA tests performed, the Palo Verde seed pods found in the rear of the truck came from the Palo Verde tree at the scene of the crime. Further, he noted that these seeds could not have come from any of the other twelve PaloVerde trees in the area. He was able to distinguish each of the twelve trees from one another based on their unique DNA. Further, although he was supplied samples from each tree, he was not told which sample came from the tree with the abrasion until after his tests were completed and his report written. Also, Dr. Helentjaris tested an additional nineteen Palo Verde trees collected from around the county. He was able to distinguish one tree from another. As it turned out, Palo Verde trees are highly distinctive in their DNA patterns.

The defendant was convicted by a jury of murder and his conviction was affirmed on appeal on April 11, 1995. This was the first case where RAPD was approved for forensic use. Even the defense expert testified that he used RAPD in his laboratory. His only criticism was that it was not as powerful as RFLP. Dr. Helentjaris testified to a random match of one in a million. The defense expert offered odds of one in 136,000.

In *Arizona v. Johnson*, 1995 WL 328780, the Division 2 Court of Appeals, affirmed the conviction of the defendant for forcible rape. In this state conducted DNA RFLP tests there was a five probe match. The random match of 1 in 312 million was calculated using the NRC ceiling method of calculation. The court distinquished *Bible* and *Hummert* by noting that in this case, there was no question raised concerning the reliability of the testing process, but only the statistical computations. The court noted that *Bible* and *Hummert* refused admission of the DNA evidence on the grounds that the method of calculating the frequencies was not generally accepted in the scientific community and, therefore, failed to meet *Frye*. In the present case, the court noted that the method of calculating frequencies was conducted pursuant to the ceiling principle set forth in the 1992 NRC report. The court ruled that this method meets *Frye*. Accordingly, the court affirmed the admission of DNA evidence and the statistical probabilities. But see *Arizona v. Boles*, 1995 WL 456229 (Ct. of App. August 3, 1995), where the court reversed the conviction of the defendant on the grounds that the experts opinion went beyond the mere expression that a match means that two DNA samples are consistent with coming from the same person. The expert failed to note that it does not mean that it necessarily comes from the same person. Statistics are not admissible.

§ 3 ARKANSAS:

In *Prater v. Arkansas*, 307 Ark. 180, 820 S.W.2d 429 (1991), a rape case, the court admitted a FBI generated RFLP test under a relevancy approach of *Arkansas Rules of Evidence* 401, 402, 702 and *United States v. Downing*, 753 F.2d 1224 (3d. Cir. 1985), which requires the following standard: (1) the reliability of the novel process used to generate the evidence, (2) the possibility that the evidence would overwhelm, confuse or mislead the jury, and (3) the connection between the evidence and the disputed factual issues in the case. Under the first prong, Arkansas adopted a standard that requires the proponent of the evidence to establish that the laboratory followed correct protocol and that the process underlying the statistical estimate of a random match is valid.

The court noted that the offered estimate of 1 in 3700 is not essential to DNA identification, but, given the impact of this type of evidence, the court indicated that it was not declaring that such evidence was *per se* admissible. The court found that the FBI's fixed bin methodology (i.e., assigning 20 bins for each of its 4 probes and calculating allele frequency by dividing the total number of alleles falling within a particular bin by the total number of alleles resulting from the profiling of all samples for that probe) to be sufficiently conservative to correct any deviation from Hardy-Weinberg equilibrium in its database. However, the court emphasized that, in evaluating this particular issue in the future:

> "[u]pon reviewing the foregoing evidence, we cannot say that the trial court abused its discretion in admitting the calculations as to probabilities. However, just because there was no meaningful attack upon the population genetics in this case does not mean that there cannot be a successful attack in future cases...Just how small the sample population may be, how the sampling is done, and the assumptions that underlie the probability calculation from the sample may all be the subject of dispute. In short the population criterion against which DNA identification matches are declared is not a closed issue"
> (820 S.W.2d at 439).

See *Swanson v. Arkansas*, 308 Ark. 28, 823 S.W.2d 812 (1992). See also, *Hunter v. Arkansas*, 875 S.W.2d. 63 (Ark. Sup. Ct. 1994).

§ 4 CALIFORNIA:

The law of California reflects some disagreement on the part of the intermediate appellate courts. However, the most recent cases seem to agree with each other.

In *California v. Wilds*, 37 Cal.Rptr.2d 351 (Cal. App. 2d Dist. 1995), the Court of Appeals again reviewed DNA forensic evidence. The facts of the case are noteworthy.

On December 6, 1986, the first victim was waiting for an elevator in the basement garage of her apartment complex when a black male wearing a mask made of "stretchy" material put a knife to her neck and asked for money. The victim gave him her purse. He forced her to a locked room in the garage, ordered her to disrobe and raped her and forced her to commit sodomy. At trial, some two years later, she could only say that the defendant "resembled" her assailant.

On February 21, 1987, another young woman was getting out of her car in the basement garage of her building, when a black male wearing a mask made of a "knit-like" material, put a knife to her throat and asked for her purse. It was in her car, she said. The man then forcibly raped her and compelled oral sodomy. He took her purse and other personal property from her car.

On April 2, 1987, a third young woman was pulling into the underground garage of her apartment complex when she saw the defendant entering her garage. She became frightened, drove out of the garage and called the police.

A short distance from the garage, the police observed the defendant who matched the description given, riding a bicycle. He was taken into custody and a knife was found beside the bicycle. He was taken to the precinct and told to remove his clothes. While he was taking off his pants, a nylon stocking fell to the floor. He said he had it to wear on his head.

On April 3, 1987, the police searched the defendant's apartment. The search uncovered a gym bag taken during the rape and robbery which occurred on February 21, 1987. A further search uncovered a necklace which was forcibly taken during the December 27, 1986 robbery.

Vaginal aspirates (a vaginal wash which removes cells) were performed after each rape which resulted in the retrieval of sperm cells from each of the victims. DNA tests indicated that the DNA in these sperm cells were identical. The defendant's blood was obtained and DNA testing demonstrated that the DNA extracted from the defendant's blood matched the DNA profile of the sperm cells extracted from each of the victims. The odds of anyone else depositing the sperm specimens were estimated to be 1 in 4.5 million.

This was a Cellmark generated RFLP test. Seventeen experts testified. Eight for the prosecution and eight for the defense. One expert testified for both sides.

This appellate court, in an extensive review of all the troubling issues that have been raised concerning DNA forensic evidence, ruled that DNA forensic evidence meets the California standard of admissibility. In evaluating the defense witness concerning sub-populations, the court quoted the prosecution expert:

> "Conneally was of the opinion that Mueller was 'making mountains out of molehills from a scientific point of view.'"
> *Supra*, p. 357.

Referring to the 1992 NRC report, the court noted that the NRC indicated that a substructuring controversy existed, but the report made no effort to resolve the controversy. Indeed, the court noted the report assumed "for the sake of discussion" that substructuring existed. The court, in analyzing *Barney* and *Axell*, concluded that this split in authority was "more perceived than real." Recent developments by renowned scientists, including Dr. Eric Lander and Dr. Bruce Budowle, clearly "demonstrate that the decision in *Axell* was correct." *supra*, p. 359. (For a further discussion of these issues see *California v. Soto*, and *California v. Amundson*, analyzed hereafter.) The court also noted that Dr. Chakraborty, Dr. Kidd and the recently completed five volume report of the FBI, produced "hard data" proving there was no substructuring which would affect the product rule. The court concluded that:

> "Even exercising the greatest possible restraint, it is apparent that...RFLP DNA profiling has achieved 'a consensus drawn from a typical cross-section of the relevant, qualified scientific community.'" *Supra*, p. 360.

For similar rulings and the most recent discussions see *California vs. Taylor*, 33 Cal. App. 4th 636 (Court of Appeals, 4th Circuit, decided March 21, 1995); *California v. Marlow*, 41 Cal.Rptr.2nd 5 (Court of Appeals, 6th Circuit, decided April 25, 1995); *California v. Burks*, 1995 WL 464138 (Ct. of App. 4th Cir., decided August 7, 1995 and modified on September 6, 1995, accepting the "modified ceiling" principal 1995 WL 527246).

In *California v. Soto*, 30 Cal. App. 4th 340, 35 Cal.Rptr.2d. 846

(1994)(Petition for review granted 890 P.2d 1115, 39 Cal.Rptr.2d 406) (March 16, 1995), the defendant was convicted of attempted rape of an elderly woman. The victim made a prompt outcry immediately after the attack giving some details, but shortly thereafter suffered a severe and debilitating stroke. The defendant was arrested based on the victim's statement. A semen stain was recovered from the victim's bedspread and DNA RFLP testing produced a match to the defendant's DNA profile. Because of the stroke, the victim was unable to testify at trial. Hence, the DNA evidence was the major evidence against the defendant.

The appellate court affirmed the trial court's admission into evidence of an Orange County Sheriff's Department laboratory generated RFLP test which showed a match along four chromosomes and which admitted into evidence statistical numbers generated by the "product rule" and the FBI's fixed bin and the floating bin methods. The fixed bin generated figures of one in a 189 million Hispanics and one in 38 million Caucasians. The floating bin generated probabilities of one in 6.7 billion persons (there were six hundred thousand comparisons made). It was noted by the court that the Orange County laboratory did not account for sub-populations. The court also noted the testimony of Dr. Kenneth Kidd, director of the Yale University DNA lab and an executive of the Human Genome Mapping Project, that the "product rule" can be applied because the frequency determination derived from it is still as accurate as any determination can possibly be:

> "Although the greater the database the greater the certainty of the estimate, *any difference in estimates over one in a million becomes pragmatically meaningless.*" (emphasis added).[59]

The court also cited the article *DNA Fingerprinting Dispute Laid to Rest*, 371 Nature 735 (October 27, 1994), by former antagonists, Dr. Eric Lander and Dr. Bruce Budowle. The court noted with approval that there is no legal barrier for introducing both the higher probability numbers generated by the "product rule" and the lower numbers generated by the use of the "ceiling principle." The court further noted:

> "Most importantly, the scientists themselves now proclaim 'the DNA Fingerprinting wars are over'" (Lander and Budowle, *supra*, p. 735).

Although the court in *California v. Axell*, 235 Cal. App.3d 836, 1 Cal.Rptr.2d 411 (2d Dist. 1991), found that a Cellmark generated RFLP test was reliable and admissible, the court in *California v. Barney*, 8 Cal.App.4th 798, 10 Cal.Rptr.2d 731 (1992), criticized *Axell* as not reflecting the current state of scientific discord. A review of the facts in *Barney* is instructive. The defendant accosted the victim at knifepoint as she was entering her car in the parking lot of the metro transit system. He forced her to drive from the area, subsequently sexually assaulting her in the car, ejaculating on her clothing. He stole her car keys, money and metro fare card. Being eventually presumed innocent, but certainly not intelligent, the defendant dropped his wallet in the car which contained a photo identification card. The victim identified the defendant from this card. The defendant was arrested at the address listed on the card recovered at the scene. Upon the defendants arrest, a metro fare card minus the exact fare necessary to travel from the scene of the attack to the defendant's home, a knife and money of the victim were recovered. The victim later identified her metro card, the knife and the defendant.

DNA testing of the semen found on the victim's clothing matched the defendant's DNA profile.

The *Barney* court found that both Cellmark and FBI generated RFLP tests were inadmissible due to their use of the product rule and the lack of scientific agreement supporting it. In *California v. Pizarro*, 10 Cal.App. 4th 57, 12 Cal. Rptr.2d 436 (1992), the court also rejected an FBI generated RFLP test under their *Frye/Kelly* (*California v. Kelly*, 17 Cal.3d 24 [Cal Sup. Ct. 1976]) standard due to an insufficient showing that FBI protocols are generally regarded as reliable. Here testimony was offered by a single witness who had been with the FBI lab since its inception. The court found that a similar showing was deemed inadequate in *California v. Brown*, 40 Cal.3d 512, 533 (Cal.Sup. Ct. 1985). See also *California v. Wallace*, 14 Cal. App. 4th 651, 17 Cal.Rptr. 2d 721 (1993); *California v. Venegas*, 31 Cal. App. 4th 234, 36 Cal.Rptr. 2d 836 (1995).

The court in *Pizzaro* refused to follow *California v. Axell, supra,* because that decision reviewed a Cellmark generated test. The court stated that it would not use authority regarding Cellmark to validate FBI generated evidence. The court also refused to accept the FBI's statistical database for Blacks when the defendant in the case before it was a member of a subgroup (Blacks of Nigerian descent). The court stated that:

> "It is evident that there is no generally accepted scientific theory on population genetics involving broad racial and ethnic groups as opposed to the argument of substructure. We cannot resolve on this record the question of general acceptance in the scientific community. We

conclude on the present record that the admission of the
RFLP test results together with the statistical conclusions
drawn therefrom was error."

In *California v. Mack*, Sacramento Cty. Super. Ct., No. 86116, 9/19/90
(PCR), the trial court refused admission of PCR DQ Alpha despite the testimony of seven expert witnesses for the prosecution, relying on the single
dissenting expert offered by the defense. Despite the defendant's testimony admitting sexual intercourse with the victim, which corroborated the PCR DQ Alpha
results, the court stated:

> "I think it is impressive, and it is undisputed that the
> technology in question is being used in the medical con-
> text and in a number of important areas to diagnose the
> number of genetically based diseases like sickle-cell ane-
> mia, Tay-Sachs. It is used to detect genetic diseases in
> fetuses. Significant decisions are made based upon those
> applications. I am not convinced, however, that there is
> a need in those contexts for the same degree of reliabili-
> ty as required in this context."

In *California v. Moffitt*, San Diego Cty. Superior Ct., No. CR 1030-94,
5/21/91, the court intensely criticized *Mack* in a scathing analysis. The court
held:

> "It is amazing to me that even though life and death
> decisions are being made daily utilizing this particular
> form of testing that the judge in the *Mack* case deemed it
> appropriate to state that in the criminal law the standard
> must go beyond that acceptable in the medical, scientific
> and research communities. I don't even understand that.
> Especially when one looks at the type of evidence that is
> admissible in trials, all trials of all kinds, it is hard for me
> to believe that a system that is used daily by parents to
> determine whether or not to allow a fetus to live or die is
> somehow a standard that we should set aside or disre-
> gard. With all due respect to my colleague in the *Mack*
> case, I resoundingly disagree."

See *California v. Bravo*, 23 Cal.Rptr.2d 48 (Cal.App. 2d Dist. 1993); *California
v. Littleton*, 7 Cal.App.4th 906, 9 Cal.Rptr.2d 288 (1992). For a discussion of

the use of statistics in a non-DNA criminal case, see *California v. Peneda*, 38 Cal.Rptr.2d. 312 (Cal.App. 4th Dist. 1995).

In *California v. McSherry*, 14 Cal.Rptr. 2d 630, (Cal. App.2d Dist. 1992), DNA identification evidence generated through PCR was admitted pursuant to the defendant's application in a post-trial hearing. However, it was found to be insufficient to warrant a new trial. A PCR DQ-Alpha test excluded the defendant. Both the rape complainant and defendant were type 1.2, 4. Dr. Edward Blake, who originated the PCR test and conducted this analysis, found that the semen in the victim's underwear was type 4.4 based on his failure to detect the 1.2 allele, however. The counter experts indicated that the failure to detect the 1.2 allele could result from degradation or contamination of the sample by bacteria or by foreign cells exaggerated by PCR analysis. There was a probability of contamination of the panties which were already soiled and contained fecal matter. There was extremely strong eyewitness testimony in the case.

Finally, in *California v. Amundson*, 41 Cal. Rptr.2d 127, 34 Cal. App. 4th 1151, decided on May 9, 1995, the same appellate panel which declared that DNA forensic evidence failed to meet *Kelly/Frye* in the 1991 *Barney* case, was once again confronted with a Cellmark generated RFLP DNA test. There was a four probe match generating statistics of 1 in 340 million Caucasians, 1 in 100 million African-Americans and 1 in 270 million Western Hispanics. Further, PCR DQ-Alpha testing was conducted by Serological Research Institute on the semen recovered from the vaginal cavity of the victim and compared with the defendant's DNA profile. The results indicated that the only 3.9 percent of the Caucasian population, 6.9 percent of the African-American population and .3 percent of the Hispanic population had these genetic markers which also matched the defendant's. The court was called upon to determine if this method of DNA testing met the *Kelly/Frye* standard of admissibility. The court affirmed the admission of both tests, noting:

> "Since *Barney* was decided the scientific landscape has once again changed... In light of the FBI study, the recent scientific literature and judicial decisions from other jurisdictions, we have come full circle...Because this evidence satisfies *Kelly*, the court properly admitted it at trial."

§ 5 COLORADO:

In *Fishback v. Colorado*, 851 P.2d 884 (Colo. Sup.Ct. 1993) (*en banc*), the Supreme Court of Colorado affirmed the defendant's conviction for rape where the facts proven included fingerprints of the defendant found at the scene and the victim's identification shortly after the attack. Vaginal sperm recovered matched the defendant's DNA profile.

The court found that a Cellmark generated RFLP test was admissible under *Frye* and *Colorado v. Anderson*, 637 P.2d 354 (Colo. Sup. Ct. 1981), which requires proof of (1) general acceptance in the relevant scientific community of the underlying theory or principle and (2) general acceptance in the relevant scientific community of the techniques used to apply that theory or principle at the time that the evidence was offered at trial. The court found that both the theory and the technique of DNA RFLP are generally accepted. Further, questions relating to the accuracy of the particular test go to the weight of the evidence. In the future, trial courts may take judicial notice of the acceptance of these issues. Cellmark's calculations, using the "product rule" resulting in a random match of 1 in 830 million was found to be generally accepted in 1989. The question of whether this conclusion remains valid in light of the substructure controversy remains for future trial courts to determine. See *Colorado v. Lindsey*, 868 P.2d 1085 (Colo. Ct. App. 1993), *Aff'd.* 1995 WL 92778 (1995); *Colorado v. Groves*, 854 P.2d 1310 (Colo. Ct. App. 1992).

§ 6 CONNECTICUT:

The skilled forensic investigation in *Connecticut v. Sivri*, 231 Conn. 115, 646 A.2d 169 (1994), deserves attention.

The defendant was convicted of murdering a 21 year old woman in his home. The victim was a masseuse who went exclusively to customers' homes. The defendant called for a masseuse at the victim's place of employment, supplying his name, address and telephone number. The victim was assigned to service the defendant at his home and traveled there in her Volkswagon. Her car was observed at the defendant's home by a witness. When the victim did not call her employer at the end of the session, which was the practice, the police were called. They responded to the defendant's home and found no one there. Both the Volkswagon and the defendant's car were gone. The victim's unoccupied car was later discovered. Eventually, the defendant returned to his home and upon questioning by the police, admitted seeing the victim, claiming he paid her and then she left. A search warrant was obtained and a search of the defendant's home took place three days later. Accompanying the police was Dr. Henry Lee, a prominent forensic scientist and director of the state forensic laboratory.

Blood stains and splatter were noted in his home. Subsequent testing proved it to be the same blood type as the victim. Also noted was human tissue in a garbage can in the garage and blood droplets leading from the house to the garage. Blood wipings on the wall of the family room were consistent with someone trying to clean off the blood from the walls. Multiple other blood spots were discovered throughout the rooms and upon various objects. Dr. Lee, noticing that the carpet in the family room was damp and discolored, proceeded to cut the carpet to expose its underside and the padding. The underside of the carpet and the padding revealed a huge section of fresh red blood. This indicated that a massive amount of blood saturated the surface of the carpet, seeping through to the underside of the carpet and soaking the padding underneath. The blood appeared to be dispersed on the surface of the carpet by a liquid containing soap. Tests proved merely that it was human blood. However, the massive amount of blood observed indicated that a person lost up to one quarter of the total blood volume in the person's body. Dr. Lee's observations of the blood splattering throughout the premises indicated that a mechanical force was used to project the blood in small randomly distributed patterns. The victim's earring was also found on the rug. Hair belonging to the victim was obtained from a hairbrush from her residence and compared to hair found in the carpet. It produced a similar match.

The defendant's abandoned truck, without plates, was discovered one week after the victim's disappearance. Blood was found on the steering wheel, floor of the trunk, interior panels of the truck and on the rear bumper. Inside the vehicle was a bag containing Pine Sol and two unused sponges. The truck carpet had been removed.

On the day the defendant's home was to be searched, the defendant quit his job and traveled to Turkey explaining to his friends at work that he had vague "personal problems." The defendant returned to New York some three months later. He was arrested by the FBI while using an alias.

The victim's body was never found. Therefore, DNA testing of the victim's parents was conducted to establish that the victim was their child and thus the victim's identity. The DNA profile obtained from the blood found at the scene was compared to the DNA profile of the suspected victim's mother and father. The DNA profile of the crime scene blood matched three bands of the mother and three bands of the father, thereby establishing maternity and paternity. The experts concluded the deceased was the missing masseuse [*See Figure 10*].

The defendant was convicted despite the fact that there was a lack of direct evidence, to wit:

1) No body or body parts were ever found
2) No weapon was recovered
3) No evidence of how or where wounds were inflicted

The court observed that the circumstantial evidence was compelling, noting:

1) Large volume of blood supports the inference of where the wound was inflicted
2) Evidence indicates that the wound was caused by a weapon
3) Large volume of blood supports the inference that the weapon deeply cut a blood vessel
4) Failure of the defendant to call for medical assistance
5) There was an attempt to destroy bloody evidence
6) The flight of the defendant to Turkey
7) Use of an alias upon his secret return to the U.S.
8) The DNA evidence connecting the blood in the defendant's premises to the deceased and connecting the deceased to the defendant's call for a masseuse
9) The abandoned vehicles of both the deceased and the defendant

This case also represents the significant confusion engendered by the use of statistics. The court reversed the judgment, remanded this matter for a new trial and directed that, upon a rehearing, the trial court must consider the 1992 NRC report and any other relevant evidence, including expert testimony, and whether the statistical analysis meets the appropriate scientific evidence standards.

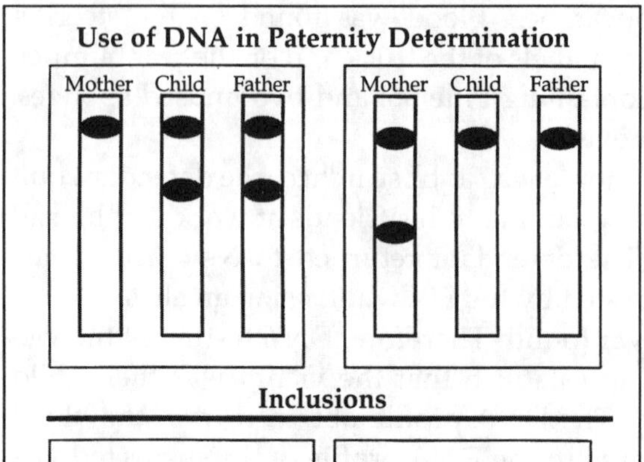

Subsequent to the reversal of the first trial and shortly before the commencement of the second trial in April, 1995, a skeleton consisting of a skull containing a bullet hole along with an intact jaw bone and teeth was discovered in a wooded area not far from where the defendant's abandoned truck was found three years earlier.

At the re-trial, both sides conceded that Cellmark's new statistical estimates were calculated in conformity with the ceiling principle. The experts still concluded that the

Figure 10

deceased was the daughter of the two parents. Additionally, a forensic orthodontist testified that the jaw and teeth attached to the skull, when compared to prior dental records of the deceased, clearly demonstrated a match. In June, 1995, the defendant was once again convicted by a jury. It is interesting to note that the new forensic orthodontic evidence supported the conclusions of the DNA experts offered at both trials.

In *Connecticut v. Zollo*, 654 A.2d 359 (Conn. App. 1995), the court affirmed the defendant's conviction for kidnapping and rape. The defendant entered the home of his estranged wife wearing a ski mask. He grabbed her at knifepoint, put a bag over her head, wrapped her head in duct tape and sexually assaulted her for about one and a half hours. A neighbor saw the defendant leave the area while wearing a knit cap which he was adjusting as he drove away. Prior to the assault, the defendant told his friend that he was going to get revenge on his wife because she initiated the separation and requested his friend to help him rape his wife, but he refused. A towel stained with semen was recovered. The victim could not identify her assailant.

In an FBI generated DNA RFLP test, comparing the DNA profile on the semen with the defendant's DNA profile, the expert for the FBI was permitted to testify that, in this four probe match, the defendant "was the likely source of the semen." In addition, statistical probabilities generated by the FBI "binning" method were allowed. The court affirmed the trial court's admission of both the opinion and the statistical evidence despite the failure to use the "ceiling" method as advocated by the NRC. This case appears to be in conflict with the ruling in *Sivri*.

§ 7 DELAWARE:

In *Delaware v. Pennell*, 584 A.2d 513 (De. Sup. Ct. 1989), the court found admissible a Cellmark generated RFLP test, under DE. Rules of Evidence 403, 702, which requires that:
1) the scientific opinion be reliable
2) the processes and tests used are reasonably relied upon by experts in the field
3) the evidence will assist the fact-finder
4) it will not create unfair prejudice or mislead the jury.

(See *Santiago v. Delaware*, 510 A.2d 488) (Del. Sup. Ct. 1986). The court refused to follow *Minnesota v. Schwartz*, 447 N.W.2d 422 (Minn. Sup. Ct. 1989) (discussed *infra* at Section 21), which ruled a Cellmark generated RFLP inadmissible because that court employed a *Frye* standard. The Delaware court refused to admit an estimate of the likelihood of a random match of 1 in 180 billion because:

1) it found an excess of homozygotes in Cellmark's database, which it found may be due to Cellmark's use of a 20 cm. gel that allows smaller alleles to run off the end of the gel

2) Cellmark's use of two "resolution units" to define a match where two gels are examined, notwithstanding the fact that its database contains data taken from single gel tests in which just one "resolution unit" was used to define a match. The court adhered to this opinion after hearing reargument based upon further work by Cellmark using a 15 cm. gel and a new database because the product rule generated such a large number that it would unduly influence the jury. See *Nelson v. Delaware*, 628 A.2d 69 (Del. Sup.Ct. 1993) *affirming* 1991 WL 190308 (Del. Super. Ct. 1991).

§ 8 THE DISTRICT OF COLUMBIA:

In *United States v. Porter*, 618 A.2d 629 (D.C. Ct.App. 1992), the court found that the FBI's statistical estimate of a random match of 1 in 30 million was unreliable in view of controversy surrounding use of the product rule as reflected in: (1) two articles which appeared in one issue of *Science* magazine, one by Lewontin and Hartl, entitled *Population Genetics in Forensic DNA Typing*, 254 *Science* 1745 (12/20/91), and the second by Chakraborty and Kidd, entitled *The Utility of DNA Typing in Forensic Work*, 254 *Science* 1735 (12/20/91); and (2) the April 1992 report of the National Academy of Sciences Committee on DNA Technology in Forensic Science; and (3) *California v. Barney*, 8 Cal.App. 4th 798, 10 Cal. Rptr. 731 (1992) (discussed *supra* at Section 4).

Relying on *People v. Mohit*, 153 Misc.2d 22 (West. Co. Ct. 1992) (discussed *infra*, at Section 29(a)), however, the court concluded that a more conservative estimate of the likelihood of a purely random match would be admissible, and it remanded the case for further hearings on this matter.

Upon rehearing, the court held that the "ceiling principle" to calculate probabilities as set forth by the 1992 NRC report has gained acceptance and is admissible. See *United States v. Porter*, 1994 WL 742297 (D.C. Super. Ct. November 17, 1994). See also *Hagins v. United States*, 639 A.2d. 612 (D.C. Ct. App. 1994).

§ 9 FLORIDA:

In *Brim v. Florida*, 1995 WL 92712 (1995), 20 Fla. Law Weekly D628, the Second District Court of Appeals affirmed the rape convictions of the defen-

dant and the sentence of life in prison. The defendant was convicted of raping two separate victims. DNA evidence, recovered from the semen in both
victims, was compared with the defendant's DNA profile and matched.
Distinguishing the *Vargas* case, the court held that RFLP DNA tests conducted by the Florida Department of Law Enforcement was admissible
along with their statistical calculations of 1 in 4 billion. The defendant's estimates of 1 in 9000 is also admissible. The testing laboratory followed the FBI
protocol. The court reasoned that there can be more than one deduction
from generally accepted theories. The court noted:

> "As Albert Einstein said, 'One reason why mathematics
> enjoys special esteem, above all other sciences, is that its
> laws are absolutely certain and indisputable, while those
> of all other sciences are to some extent debatable...'Indeed,
> no scientific advance has yet been developed that cannot
> be questioned or debated. For this reason, evidentiary
> rules do not require absolute certainty or unanimity."

In *Vargas v. Florida*, 640 So.2d 1139 (Fla. Dist. Ct. App. 1994) the Court
concluded that the method used to calculate the population frequency statistics was not generally accepted in the relevant scientific community.
Expert testimony indicated that a more conservative method, as recommended by the 1992 NRC report, was the appropriate method which would
account for the possibility of population substructure. Therefore, the case
was remanded to the trial court to determine if the more conservative
approach of calculating population frequencies was generally accepted and,
if so, whether the DNA evidence would be admissible.

In *Olvera v. Florida*, 641 So.2d 120 (Fla. Dist. Ct. App. 1994), the appellate
court affirmed the FBI generated RFLP test and the use of its "binning"
method on the grounds that the defendant failed to challenge these issues in
the lower court, thereby distinguishing the *Vargas* case, *supra*.

In *Crews v. Florida*, 644 So.2d 338 (Fla. Dist. Ct. App. 1994), the appellate
court affirmed the defendant's conviction based, in part, on DNA evidence
and statistical probabilities on the grounds that the defendant failed to properly object to the introduction of the evidence. The court distinguished
Vargas, *supra*, on the grounds that *Vargas* specifically objected to the basis of
the population frequencies. The rehearing decision in *Vargas* has not yet
been decided.

In *Andrews v. Florida*, 533 So.2d 841 (Fla. Ct. App. 1988), *rev. den.* 542
So.2d 1332 (Fla. Sup. Ct. 1989), the defendant was convicted of rape and
other charges. Although the victim could not identify her attacker, finger-

prints lifted inside the premises matched the defendant's right index and middle finger. A vaginal swab recovered sperm. The DNA profile of the defendant matched the profile on the recovered sperm.

The court admitted a Lifecode's RFLP test and its estimate of 1 in 839 million under a relevancy standard (although it noted that the evidence would be admissible under a *Frye* standard as well). The court reasoned that RFLP has been used for ten years by scientists and accepted expert testimony that, if an error occurs, RFLP will generate no result rather than the wrong result (Contra, *People v. Castro*, 144 Misc.2d 956, 973-974 n.7, n.8).

In a second case, *Martinez v. Florida*, 549 So.2d 694 (Fla. Ct. App. 1989), the Florida court admitted a Lifecodes' generated RFLP test and its statistical estimate of a random match of 1 in 234 billion where the defense did not attempt to refute the scientific basis the test or the basis for the statistical estimate.[60] See *Florida v. Wyatt*, 641 So.2d 1336 (Fla. Sup. Ct. 1994); *Robinson v. Florida*, 610 So.2d 1288 (Fla. Sup. Ct. 1992). See also *Brim v. Florida*, 1995 WL 92712 (Fla. Dist. Ct. App. 1995). In *Cade v. Florida*, 1995 WL 326107, 20 Fla. L. Weekly D1335, decided June 2, 1995, the court reversed the defendant's conviction on the grounds that the trial court should have granted the defendant's request for a State appointed DNA expert.

The Florida Supreme Court in *Hayes v. Florida*, 1995 WL 368405 (June 26, 1995), reversed the defendants conviction and death sentence. The court found that Lifecode's methods for correcting "band shifting" was not accepted in the scientific community or the 1992 NRC report. The court held that where "band shifting" occurs, there should be an "inconclusive" result reported. The court did note that DNA forensic testing does meet *Frye* if the laboratory uses scientifically accepted procedures.

§ 10 GEORGIA:

In *Caldwell v. Georgia*, 260 Ga. 278, 393 S.E.2d 436 (1990), the defendant was charged with murder and the prosecution sought the death penalty. There was a pre-trial DNA hearing which was appealed by the defendant after an adverse ruling by the trial court.

The gruesome facts of this case indicate that the mother of two children arrived home to discover that her children had been brutally stabbed. The police were called and upon arrival, discovered the body of a twelve-year-old. Also found was a ten-year-old stabbed numerous times and close to death, but alive. The defendant disappeared shortly after these events. The police seized the defendant's bloody clothes found at the premises. The defendant's truck was found abandoned in some woods shortly thereafter. The bloodstains on the defendant's clothes matched the DNA profile of the children. The estimates offered were 1 in 24 million. The defense offered frequencies of 1 in 250,000.

The court declared a Lifecodes' generated RFLP test to be admissible under the standard of *Harper v. Georgia*, 249 Ga. 519, 292 S.E.2d 389 (1982), which rejects the *Frye* standard as "counting heads" and admits evidence if the:

> "technique in question has reached a scientific stage of verifiable certainty or...rests upon the laws of nature...The trial court makes this determination based upon the evidence available to him rather than by simply calculating the consensus in the scientific community" (*supra*, p. 411).

For *Harper* admissibility, the *Caldwell* court adopted a requirement that the proponent of the evidence must show that the laboratory "substantially performed the scientific procedures in an acceptable manner." (393 S.E.2d at 441).

Thereafter the defendant was tried for murder and convicted. The jury did not impose the death penalty and the defendant was sentenced to life imprisonment. The Supreme Court of Georgia affirmed the admission of DNA forensic evidence and the conviction. *Caldwell v. Georgia*, 263 Ga. 560, 436 S.E.2d. 488 (1993). See *Johnson v. Georgia*, 448 S.E.2d 177 (Ga. Sup. Ct. 1994) *aff'd.* after remand hearing, 1995 WL 534595 September 11, 1995; *Morris v. Georgia*, 212 Ga. App. 42, 441 S.E.2d 273 (1994).

In *Blige v. Georgia*, 221 Ga.App. 771, 440 S.E.2d 521 (1994), the victim was asleep on a couch in her residence at 3:00 A.M. when awakened by a man standing over her who was touching her. He forced her off the couch into the bedroom where he raped her. Because of the similarities in this incident and other rapes admittedly committed by the defendant, he immediately became a suspect. Semen recovered from the victim was compared with the defendant's blood and there was a genetic match, with a probability calculation ranging from 1 in 3 trillion to 1 in 130 million to 1 in 8 million. The court affirmed the conviction of rape and adopted the rulings in *Caldwell*, *supra.*, in affirming the trial court's admission of DNA evidence. *Accord*, *Hornsby v. Georgia*, 210 Ga. App. 571, 436 S.E.2d 767 (1993); *Nichols v. Georgia*, 210 Ga. App. 134, 435 S.E.2d 502 (1993); *Greenway v. Georgia*, 207 Ga. App. 511, 428 S.E.2d 415 (1993); *Smith v. Georgia*, 1995 WL 418718 (Ga. Sup. Ct., July 14, 1995). *Accord, Redding v. Georgia*, 1995 WL 648901 (Ga. Ct. App. November 6, 1995) (RFLP, PCR & D1S80)

§ 11 HAWAII:

In *Hawaii v. Montalbo*, 828 P.2d 1274 (Haw. Sup. Ct. 1992), the court found that an FBI generated RFLP test and its estimate that the likelihood of a random match would be in 1 in 1000 for Hispanics, to be admissible under the *Frye* standard, as encompassed by *Hawaii v. Kim*, 64 Haw. 598, 645 P.2d 1330 (1982) and *Haw. Rules of Evidence* 702, 703. The court rejected the defendant's arguments directed toward the statistical estimate by noting:

> "We find little basis for concern over the theory underlying the statistical evidence. It suffices to say that statistics and the underlying sampling theory are not novel or controversial. We take judicial notice that the DNA paradigm is not controversial and is widely accepted in the relevant scientific community. We also recognize that the basic techniques underlying the analysis used by the FBI are widely accepted" (*supra*, p. 1281).
>
> "[W]e conclude that the court did not abuse its discretion in determining that the statistical evidence was a reasonable estimate of population frequencies, and reliable enough to admit into evidence. If valid, defendant's objections would go to the weight rather that the admissibility of the evidence at trial" (Id. at 1282).

§ 12 ILLINOIS:

In *Illinois v. Watson*, 257 Ill.App.3d 915, 629 N.E.2d 634, 196 Ill.Dec. 89 (1994), the trial court's order granting defendant's motion to exclude the DNA profiling evidence based upon the method of the statistical calculation was vacated, and the case was remanded to the trial court for further proceedings. The appellate court affirmed the trial court's finding of general acceptance of the matching technique. However, due to the recommendations of the NRC, the appellate court remanded the case to determine if the ceiling principle method of statistical calculation is appropriate under *Frye*.

The facts in *Illinois v. Stremmel*, 630 N.E.2d 1301 (Ill. App. Ct. 1994), are noteworthy. The defendant and the deceased attended AA meetings together but on the night of the murder, they were seen drinking together at various bars. The deceased was later found in his home lying in a pool of blood. Autopsy determined that death was caused by a brutal beating inflicted with a blunt instrument consistent with a tire iron. There were no eyewitnesses, fingerprints or evidence of forced entry. Bloody footprints did not match the deceased, but were subsequently determined to match the defendant's size and style shoe he usually wore. Investigation prompted by the defendant's presence with the deceased shortly before the murder led to a search of the car the defendant was driving on the night of the murder. The inspection revealed that the tire iron was missing; a blue contact lens was recovered near the passenger seat; a tiny blood stain on the brake pedal and small blood stain on the driver's seat. The deceased was wearing only one blue contact lens and the lens recovered from the defendant's car was consistent with the lens worn by the victim. DNA testing of the blood found in the car was consistent with the DNA profile of the deceased and inconsistent with the defendant's DNA profile which was also tested.

The court affirmed the defendant's murder conviction. The court found that the FBI generated RFLP testing and its "binning" method meets *Frye*. However, in its discussion, the court specifically rejected the perceived three prong *Frye* test allegedly set forth in *People v. Castro, infra.*

In *Illinois v. Heaton*, 640 N.E.2d 630 (Ill. App. Ct. 1994), the defendant's murder conviction was affirmed. The defendant's car was seen at the scene of the victim's trailer inside which her body was discovered. The defendant had known the victim since high school. Blood, hair and fiber evidence recovered from the scene could not be positively identified as coming from the defendant. Semen recovered from the deceased's pubic hair was subjected to DNA testing and matched the defendant's DNA profile.

The DNA RFLP testing conducted by the state crime lab, which produced a statistical calculation of 1 in 52,000 obtained by the use of the "product rule," met *Frye* and was reliable and admissible. The court refused to take judicial notice of the NRC report which criticized the use of the "product rule."

In *Illinois v. Lipscomb*, 215 Ill. App.3d 413, 574 N.E.2d 1345 (1991), the court held that a Lifecodes generated RFLP test was admissible under the *Frye* standard, ruling that any questions regarding specific procedures go to weight rather than admissibility. The Court noted:

> "[I]f it is shown that the procedures used give an unreliable result, then the court may find it necessary to exclude this evidence entirely." (*supra*, p. 1357)

The court admitted the statistical evidence that the likelihood of a random match would be 1 in 6.8 billion (there being about 6 billion humans on the planet). *Accord: Illinois v. Miles*, 217 Ill.App.3d 393, 577 N.E.2d 477 (1991) (Cellmark generated RFLP test). For comparison see: *Illinois v. Harbold*, 124

Ill.App.3d 363, 464 N.E.2d 734 (1984) (testimony based on blood marker frequencies excluded).

In *Illinois v. Mehlberg*, 618 N.E.2d 1168 (Ill.App. Ct. 1993) the defendant was convicted of raping his next door neighbor. The victim could not identify her attacker as he was wearing a ski mask in the darkened home, but the defendant mentioned the name of the victim's husband and knew he was previously convicted of a felony. The defendant also noted that he had been in the victim's house on a prior occasion and mentioned some of her actions and movements. These factors were sufficient to attract the attention of the police. Semen stains were recovered from the victim's underwear and on a vaginal swab. DNA testing showed a match between the DNA profiles noted in the sperm and the defendant's blood sample.

The court found that testimony from a Cellmark scientist that, based upon a population sample of 160-250 Caucasians, the frequency of the banding pattern was 1 in 12,000, coupled with testimony from the FBI's Dr. Adams that the likelihood of a random match was 1 in 1.7 million (multiplied by a factor of two because the data pool contains males and females and only males produce sperm), did not overwhelm the jury. That court concluded:

> "—[t]he statistical analysis is admissible as relevant to identification, and any challenge to its reliability goes only to the weight to be given by the jury to the evidence."

The Court further noted that without the statistical evidence,[60] the jury would have been free to speculate as to the meaning of the results found by the two laboratories. See *Illinois v. Johnson*, 262 Ill.App.3d 565, 634 N.E.2d 1285 (1994) *affirming* 1994 WL 197386 (Ill. App. Ct. May 20, 1994). See also *Illinois v. Ehlert*, 1995 WL 505014 (Ill. App. Ct. Aug. 25, 1995) (DNA maternity testing).

§ 13 INDIANA:

In *Hopkins v. Indiana*, 579 N.E.2d 1297 (Ind. Sup. Ct. 1991), the facts proved that in 1985, the defendant was an aerobics instructor at the YMCA where he made the acquaintance of the deceased. He visited her home one occasion. The husband of the deceased arrived home one evening to find his home in disarray and the contents of his wife's purse dumped on the floor. He found his wife's nude body kneeling over their bed. Her throat had been severely cut almost to the point of decapitation.

Genetic Fingerprinting:

The defendant also worked as a tree trimmer in the area and had contact with a neighbor one day before the murder. On the day of the murder, the defendant also spoke with another neighbor seeking employment. The neighbor, evidently suspicious of the defendant, wrote down a detailed description of the defendant. A third witness identified the defendant as being near the home of the deceased shortly after the murder, looking scratched, nervous and disheveled. The defendant said to this witness: "Goddamn, nothing went right. I fucked up. That bitch. I think they saw me. I got to get out of town. Do you have a gun? Can you take me out of town?" The witness refused.

The defendant did flee to Chicago after the murder where he wrote to his wife indicating that he would not go to jail. He fled from Chicago to California leaving behind a knife, which was recovered and determined to be capable of inflicting the wounds on the deceased. He subsequently moved to Oregon where he was arrested some three years later. Immediately after the murder in 1985, semen was recovered during autopsy and preserved during this three year period. It is noted that DNA forensic profiling was not yet available in 1985. By the time the defendant was arrested in 1988, DNA was actively being used in forensic work. DNA testing of the preserved three year old semen matched the DNA profile of the defendant. The defendant was convicted of felony murder.

The court affirmed the conviction and the admission of a Cellmark generated RFLP test, under the *Frye* standard. It held that disputes about the reliability of the specific test go to the weight of the evidence. *Accord: Davidson v. Indiana*, 580 N.E.2d 238 (Ind. Sup. Ct. 1991) (Once the trial court declares the witness an expert regarding DNA analysis, subsequent evaluation of that evidence goes only to its weight). *See Jenkins v. Indiana*, 627 N.E.2d 789 (Ind. Sup. Ct. 1993); *Lockhart v. Indiana*, 609 N.E.2d 1093 (Ind. S. Ct. 1993); *Woodcox v. Indiana*, 591 N.E.2d 1019 (Ind. Sup. Ct. 1992). *See also Harrison v. Indiana*, 644 N.E.2d. 1243 (Ind. Sup. Ct. 1995)(PCR and RFLP).

§ 14 IOWA:

In *Iowa v. Brown*, 470 N.W.2d 30 (Sup. Ct. 1991), the Supreme Court of Iowa admitted an RFLP test and its statistical estimate of the likelihood of a random match of 1 in several billion employing a reliability standard under Iowa Rules of Evidence 702, 703, finding that defects, if any, in the performance of the tests go to the weight of the evidence. In evaluating the argument of the defendant that the statistical estimates are so lopsided as to be prejudicial, the court noted that the jury would be unable to take the four probe match and come to "an answer with any degree of correctness." The court also observed that if the defendant's argument was accepted:

> "Indeed, it might lead to the exclusion of fingerprint evidence, which also is based on mathematical theory of probabilities that the chance of two people bearing the same fingerprint (or prints) is so infinitesimally small as to be negligible. *Martinez v. Florida*, 549 So.2d 694, 697 (Fla. 1989)."[62]

See also Iowa v. Smith, No. 4173, (Iowa District Court, Polk County, 1990). *Accord, Iowa v. Ripperger*, 514 N.W.2d 740 (Iowa Ct. App. 1994).

§ 15 KANSAS:

In *Smith v. Deppish*, 248 Kan. 217, 807 P.2d 144 (1991), the facts revealed that when the husband of the victim entered his darkened home, he saw his wife's body lying on the living room floor in a pool of blood. She was naked except for her bra which was pulled over her breasts. She was shot twice between the eyes at close range, but was still barely alive. A .22 caliber expended shell was near the body. She was removed to the hospital where she died shortly thereafter. At autopsy, a rape kit was prepared.

An investigation by the police uncovered two neighbors who had seen and heard a motorcycle at the home of the deceased at the time of the homicide.

The police compiled a list of residents that owned motorcycles and .22 caliber weapons. The defendant owned a motorcycle and a .22 caliber weapon. Each of the four people, including the defendant, who owned motorcycles and .22 caliber weapons were requested to test fire their guns to enable a comparison with the .22 caliber shell recovered at the scene. They all complied. The shell fired from the defendant's gun matched the recovered shell.

It was also established that he had visited the victim's home prior to the murder.

A search warrant was issued and a blood-stained holster was seized at the defendant's home. Forensic tests merely determined it to be human blood.

The semen recovered during autopsy from vaginal swabs, a blanket and jeans from the victim's home were compared with the defendant's DNA profile and they matched. The expert offered the opinion that:

> "...there was more than a 99 percent probability that

Smith was the contributor of the semen found on the swab."

The court affirmed the defendant's conviction of murder and rape and affirmed the admission of a Lifecodes generated RFLP test, under the *Frye* standard. *Accord: Kansas v. Dykes*, 847 P.2d 1214 (Kan. Sup. Ct. 1993); *Kansas v. Colbert*, 1995 WL 328914 (Kan. Sup Ct. 1995); *Kansas v. Haddock*, 1995 WL 246995 (Kan. Sup. Ct. 1995)(PCR); *Kansas v. Hill*, 1995 WL 328462 (Kan. Sup. Ct. 1995)(PCR).

§ 16 KENTUCKY:

There was a four probe match between the defendant's blood and the recovered semen in this FBI generated RFLP DNA test. No defense witnesses were called to dispute the DNA testing or calculations. The probabilities, in the words of the FBI expert, were that:

> "the likelihood of finding another unrelated individual from the Black population, having a DNA profile like Mr. Harris, is approximately one in eight million."

It is to be noted that the FBI used its "binning method" in calculating probabilities. *Harris v. Kentucky*, 846 S.W.2d 678 (Ky. Sup. Ct. 1992). In *Petry v. Kentucky*, the Court of Appeals reversed the defendant's conviction of rape on the grounds that the RFLP DNA test conducted by the state, was not first subjected to a *Frye* hearing, even though neither side requested such a hearing. (1995 WL 457212, decided August 4, 1995). In *Mitchell v. Kentucky*, 1995 WL 502 599, (August 24, 1995) the Supreme Court of Kentucky affirmed the admission of DNA RFLP evidence generated by both the FBI and Kentucky State Police Lab, which was admitted by the trial court after a *Daubert* hearing. The court decreed that the *Daubert* standard is the proper standard and shall be utilized in determining the admission of DNA evidence on a case by case basis.

§ 17 LOUISIANA:

In *Louisiana v. Stelly*, 645 So.2d 804 (La. Ct. App. 1994), the appellate court affirmed both the defendant's conviction for rape and the sentence of life plus forty years. The court also affirmed the trial court's admission of the DNA and statistical evidence in a Cellmark generated RFLP test.

In *Louisiana v. Brossette*, 634 So.2d 1309 (La. Ct. App. 1994), the forty year old defendant was the stepfather of the ten year old victim. He entered her room, forced her to remove her panties, placed her on a towel, and penetrated her. The youngster saw "white milky stuff" come out of the defendant's penis. He directed her to clean herself up and put toilet tissue in her panties. The next day, the youngster reported the attack to her teacher. Her panties and the towel were recovered from the clothes hamper. The youngster was later examined at the hospital. The examination revealed that she suffered a tear between her rectum and vagina, black and blue bruising along the hymen, as well as stretching of the hymenal opening. The examining doctor opined that the bruising was consistent with trauma occurring within the past 24 to 25 hours.

The DNA testing of the fluid recovered from the crotch of the panties and the towel revealed a mixture of genetic material matching both the youngster and the defendant. The defendant's conviction for aggravated rape and the DNA testing was affirmed. *Accord, Louisiana v. Charles,* 617 So.2d 895 (La. Sup. Ct. 1993). *See also Louisiana v. Wright,* 593 So.2d 759 (La. Ct. App. 1992); *Louisiana v. Spencer,* 1995 WL 79691, (LA. Ct. App. October, 4, 1995) (PCR).

§ 18 MARYLAND:

In *Cobey v. Maryland,* 80 Md. App.31, 559 A.2d 391 (Ct. of Special Appeals 1989), *cert. den.* 317 Md. 542, 565 A.2d 670 (1989), the court admitted a Cellmark generated RFLP test using the *Frye* standard. Seven experts testified for the People; none testified for the defense. The court noted that 1989 Md. Laws Ch. 430 (eff. 1990) would make DNA evidence admissible in a criminal trial to prove or disprove identity, and it cautioned:

> "[w]e make crystal clear that we are not, at this juncture, holding that DNA fingerprinting is now admissible willy-nilly in all criminal trials conducted between this date and on January 1, 1990 when 1989 Md. Laws Ch. 430 takes effect. We are merely holding that, based upon this record, Judge Ruben did not err in finding that DNA fingerprinting was generally acceptable in the scientific community and in permitting its introduction into evidence, since there was no evidence to the contrary" (*supra*, p. 398).

See Jackson v. Maryland, 92 Md. App. 304, 608 A.2d 782 (Ct. Spec. App. 1992); *Tapscott v. Maryland,* 1995 WL 511334 (Ct. Spec. App. August 31, 1995);

Keirsey v. Maryland, 1995 WL 516450 (Ct. Spec. App. September 1, 1995).

§ 19 MASSACHUSETTS:

In *Massachusetts v. Curnin*, 409 Mass. 218, 565 N.E.2d 440 (1991), the court ruled that DNA evidence from a Cellmark generated test would be admissible only if the jury heard evidence concerning the likelihood of a match. However, evidence of an exclusion was declared admissible without any need for showing the likelihood of a match (*supra*, p. 442-43 n.7). The *Curnin* case was reversed because the trial court admitted statistical estimate of 1 in 59 million without demonstration of the general acceptance or inherent rationality of the process by which Cellmark reached that conclusion. Compare *Massachusetts v. Drayton*, 386 Mass. 39, 434 N.E.2d 997 (1982) (error to admit testimony that probability of fingerprint is 1 out of 387 trillion).

Subsequently, in *Massachusetts v. Lanigan*, 413 Mass. 154, 596 N.E.2d 311 (1992), under a *Frye* standard, the court also refused to admit FBI generated RFLP test results and statistics because of the scientific controversy over the effect of population substructure on the Hardy-Weinberg equilibrium of a Caucasian database. Since there can be no evidence admitted concerning the likelihood of a match, the court reasoned, any evidence of a match is inadmissible under the rule of *Massachusetts v. Curnin, supra*. The court also refused to admit a Cellmark exclusion in the second case decided in the *Lanigan* opinion, *Massachusetts v. Breadmore*, and Breadmore Jr. In this incest case, where both defendant grandfather and co-defendant grandfather's son had sex with the complainant/granddaughter/niece at the time of conception, Cellmark excluded Breadmore, Jr. on the basis of a single probe when its protocols require two probes to determine an exclusion. The fact that the incestuous relationship made paternity difficult to determine should require the use of more probes to exclude rather than fewer, the court reasoned. See *Massachusetts v. Daggett*, 416 Mass. 347, 622 N.E.2d 272, 278 (1993) (The court, unable to reach a consensus on the admissibility of DNA evidence, ruled that even if the evidence was erroneously admitted, it was a harmless error. Unlike previous Massachusetts cases (*Curnin* and *Lanigan*) where DNA evidence was ruled inadmissible because of the use of quantitative probabilities, the experts in *Daggett* testified that "it would be highly likely that they (the two samples which had matching DNA profiles) came from the same person." Four of the five members of the five judge panel were evenly split on whether this characterization of a match was generally accepted in the scientific community. The remaining member refused to decide the admissibility issue and ruled that if there was error it was harmless.

The matter was remanded for additional evidence. Upon remand, the trial court admitted the DNA evidence and the statistical numbers generated by the use of the "ceiling principle." On appeal, *Massachusetts v. Lanigan*, 419 Mass. 15, 641 N.E.2d 1342 (1994), the appellate court held that DNA evidence meets *Frye* and that the dispute over statistics, which troubled the court initially, was resolved by the use of the "ceiling principle" recommended by the NRC. The law in Massachusetts, which was previously in turmoil, has now been finally settled and DNA evidence and statistical probabilities are admissible.

In *Massachusetts v. Vega*, 36 Mass. App. Ct. 636, 634 N.E.2d 149 (1994), the appellate court affirmed the trial court's judgment that allowed the prosecution's expert to use the "product rule." Although noting that this was error, they also took into account that the defendant independently tested the disputed material and, although results were obtained, the defense did not offer the results in evidence. It is further noted with interest that the prosecution expert, in addition to citing statistics, was permitted to state that:

> "it is unlikely that anyone other than the defendant deposited the sperm sample."

§ 20 MICHIGAN:

In *Michigan v. Adams*, 489 N.W.2d 192 (Mich. App. 1992), the court ruled that a Cellmark RFLP test was admissible under the *Davis-Frye* rule. See *Michigan v. Davis*, 343 Mich. 348, 72 N.W.2d 269 (1955). That court found that DNA identification evidence is generally accepted in the scientific community as reliable and concluded that trial courts may take judicial notice of its reliability. Nevertheless, before a trial court admits the test results into evidence, the prosecutor must establish, in each particular case, that the generally accepted laboratory procedures were followed (489 N.W.2d at 197). The court also decided that the admission of statistical evidence will not lead to an improper trial by mathematics. *Accord Michigan v. Courts*, 517 N.W.2d 785 (Mich. App. 1994); *Michigan v. Lee*, 1995 WL 444790 (Mich. Ct. App. July 21, 1995)(PCR); *Michigan v. McMillan*, 1995 WL 545551 (Mich. Ct. App. September 1, 1995)(PCR); *Michigan v. Jackson*, 1995 WL 546044 (Mich. Ct. App. September 5, 1995).

§ 21 MINNESOTA:

In *Minnesota v. Schwartz*, 447 N.W.2d 422 (Minn. Sup.Ct. 1989), the highest court of the state found that DNA typing is generally reliable under the *Frye* standard, and specifically rejected the relevance test under *Minn. Rules of Evidence* 403/702 for this type of evidence. In Minnesota, the courts will admit DNA evidence if the test is properly performed. Here, however, a Cellmark generated RFLP test was found to be inadmissible because Cellmark did not comport with the quality control guidelines established by the FBI's TWGDAM (Technical Working Group on DNA Analysis Methods) committee. (Note: TWGDAM did not establish the guidelines until after the conclusion of the hearing).

In *Minnesota v. Jobe*, 486 N.W.2d 407 (Minn. Sup. Ct. 1992), the defendant was the spurned boyfriend of the deceased. After contacting various co-workers of the victim to attempt a reconciliation, the defendant was successful in convincing the victim to at least meet him for lunch. However, the victim re-considered and cancelled the meeting. That day, the defendant purchased a knife. His car was seen at the victim's premises that evening. The victim lived alone with her 2½ year old daughter. Loud voices were heard.

When the victim failed to appear for work, a relative was contacted and went to the victim's home and entered with a spare key. The victim's body was observed in the living room draped over her bed. It would later be determined that she had been stabbed 106 times. The relative went into the child's room and discovered that the youngster was also dead, having been stabbed 56 times.

Blood was throughout the apartment, including the glass doors leading to the balcony and the balcony itself. A trail of blood on the sidewalk led to the parking lot where it ended.

The defendant failed to appear at work the next morning, reporting that he had cut his hand. The police learned of the identity of the defendant from the victim's fellow workers. Upon investigation, it was discovered that the defendant had called an ambulance the evening of the homicide and was treated at a local hospital for a cut hand.

The police placed the defendant's premises under surveillance and observed the defendant's father carry two garbage bags to a dumpster. The police retrieved the bags. Inside was a bloody rug and an empty hunting knife box. Later, investigation established that the knife was purchased by the defendant the day of the murder. Forensic experts later testified that the wounds of the deceased and her daughter and the cut on the defendant's hand was consistent with the type of knife purchased by him.

A search of the defendant's car revealed blood on the steering wheel, seat, seatbelt and radio dial. Also, there was a trail of blood leading from the car to the defendant's home. Bloody clothes were seized from the defendant's home.

Standard blood tests indicated that some of the blood found in the defendant's car and on his clothes could not be his but was consistent with the victims. Some blood spots in the deceased's apartment were consistent with the defendant's blood and could not be the victims'.

Blood found on the glass door leading from the victim's balcony, blood on the balcony and the sidewalk leading to the parking lot and the parking lot itself was consistent with the defendant and could not have come from the victims. Blood recovered from the switchplate in the victim's bathroom was consistent with the defendant and both victims.

DNA testing was also conducted on the blood sample recovered from inside the victim's home. The defendant's DNA profile matched the blood samples tested. DNA testing absolutely excluded the victims as donors of the blood, but did not exclude the defendant.

The Supreme Court affirmed the defendant's conviction of murder and found that the FBI's RFLP testing procedures met the reliability standard of *Schwartz* after a pretrial hearing devoted to that issue. Concerning future pretrial hearings, the court noted:

> "[w]hile we believe, given the evolving nature of this forensic specialty, a *Frye* hearing is still required, that hearing should focus only on whether the laboratory which did the testing was in compliance with the appropriate standards and controls. It should not be a forum for challenging the basic DNA RFLP testing procedures themselves. Challenges to the underlying scientific principles go to the weight to be *accorde*d the evidence and are properly introduced at trial." (*Id.* at 420.)

In 1993, the court evaluated statistical evidence in *Minnesota v. Johnson*, 498 N.W.2d 10 (Minn. Sup. Ct. 1993), and again concluded that a FBI RFLP test was properly admitted under the *Schwartz* test and that the defendant's counter arguments go to the weight of the evidence. It affirmed the trial court's order, under *Minnesota v. Kim*, 398 N.W.2d 544, 548 (Minn. Sup. Ct. 1987), which, in order to avoid a potentially exaggerated impact on the trier of fact in violation of *Minn. R. Evid.* 403, allowed an expert to present statistics only as to the frequency of the appearance of individual DNA chromosomes matching those found in the forensic sample. The expert was not allowed to draw any conclusions from such statistics, nor was he even allowed to speculate as to the frequency with which a DNA sample containing all the distinct chromosomes of this sample might appear in those populations.

Finally, in *Minnesota v. Alt*, 504 N.W.2d 38 (Minn. Ct. App. 1993), *aff'd* 505 N.W.2d 72 (Minn. Sup. Ct. 1993), a "band shifting" issue was presented and one intermediate Minnesota appellate court affirmed a pretrial ruling admitting an FBI RFLP test, finding that the FBI protocols and methodology meet the *Jobe* test, that "band shift" problems go to weight of the evidence. In the same opinion the court reversed that part of the pre-trial order which excluded a statistical estimate based on the "ceiling principle," allowing defendant at trial to offer evidence on this issue. That court barred non-statistical opinion testimony that the samples "match," however, allowing testimony only that the tests are consistent with the defendant being the source of the sample and that the tests do not exclude the defendant. See *Minnesota v. Bloom*, 516 N.W.2d 159 (Minn. Sup. Ct. 1994) Court held that the conservative "interim ceiling method" of calculating the probability of a random match recommended by the National Research Council justifies creation of DNA exception to the rule against admitting statistical probability evidence in criminal prosecutions and that a properly qualified expert may, if evidentiary foundation is sufficient, give an opinion as to the random match probability using the NRC's approach to statistical computation); *See also Minnesota v. Grayson*, No. K2-94-1298, 1994 WL 670312 (Minn. Dist. Ct. November 8, 1994) (PCR); *Minnesota v. Bauer*, 516 N.W.2d 174 (Minn. Sup. Ct. 1994) *affirming* 512 N.W.2d 112 (Minn. Ct. App. 1994); *Minnesota v. Perez*, 516 N.W.2d 175 (Minn. Sup. Ct. 1994); *Minnesota v. Nielson*, 467 N.W.2d 615 (Minn. Sup. Ct. 1991) (Court followed the *Schwartz* decision. Nevertheless, the court determined that any error concerning the lack of foundation relating to the introduction of DNA evidence was harmless).

§ 22 MISSISSIPPI:

In *Polk v. Mississippi*, 612 So.2d 381 (Miss. Sup. Ct. 1993), two women were found brutally stabbed to death in their home when police entered shortly after the event. While in the premises, they heard a noise in the rear of the house. Upon investigation, they found the rear screen torn away and tracks leading into a creek and re-emerging, continuing toward the defendant's house. Peering into the window, an officer observed the defendant with wet and muddy jeans and shoes.

A warrant was obtained and upon the defendant's arrest in his home, a bloody sheet and clothing were seized. The defendant had no apparent injuries or cuts on his body. Blood was noted on the defendant's underwear and blue jeans. Conventional blood tests conducted were consistent with the deceased's blood types.

DNA testing of the underwear blood matched one of the victims and excluded the defendant.

The admission of DNA evidence was affirmed along with the defendant's convictions for the two murders.

§ 23 MISSOURI:

In *Missouri v. Davis*, 814 S.W.2d 593 (Mo. Sup. Ct. 1991) [*cert. den.* 60 U.S. 3479, 112 S.Ct. 911, 116 L.Ed.2d 812 (1992) *(en banc)*], the following bizarre and tragic circumstances unfolded. In 1985, the wife of the defendant obtained an order of protection after having the defendant arrested for spousal abuse. The defendant was released on bail and told a friend, "The only way to stop a whoring bitch like that is to shoot her." To another friend he stated: "If she don't stop messing with me I'm going to blow her away." He then proceeded to purchase a 12 gauge shotgun and ammunition in a local sporting goods store. On the same day, the deceased left work in her red car, remarking that she was going home. She was never seen again.

The defendant, driving the victim's car to a neighboring town, rented an indoor storage place for the car. He purchased two new locks and two air fresheners. He placed the new locks on the storage space after placing the two air fresheners inside the car. He explained to the storage people that he was hiding the car to avoid losing it in a divorce proceeding. He told the same thing to the cabby who drove him home from the storage area.

The defendant was questioned concerning his wife's disappearance. He insisted that he did not know where she or her car was located.

As a result of the wife's disappearance, the criminal charges against the defendant were dismissed. The defendant proceeded to empty out the wife's bank account and change her insurance policy naming himself as beneficiary by forging her name. He then obtained a divorce along with the custody of their two children. Displaying a massive depth of disdain, he sought and received a judicial order requiring his missing wife to pay child support.

Some three years later, evidently feeling secure, he amazingly refused to pay the monthly storage on the car, despite repeated notices. Having defaulted, the storage space was forcibly opened and a grisly scene was revealed. The interior of the car was filled with dried blood, human tissue and bone fragments, later identified as part of a skull. Bone fragments contained residue from shot gun pellets. Littered on the floor were shotgun pellets. Blood wiping indicated that someone attempted to clean off the blood.

A search of the defendant's home uncovered a diamond ring always worn by the deceased that came from a previous marriage. The shotgun purchased by the defendant on the day of the victim's disappearance was discovered. Tests proved it had been fired.

Because the wife's body was never found, DNA testing of the dried blood found in the car was compared with the DNA profile of the two children, Robbie and Angela.

The results of these DNA tests established the basis of the expert opinion which was as follows:

1. It was 510 times more likely that the dried blood samples from the car came from the mother of Robbie.
2. It was 190,000 times more likely that the said dried blood came from the mother of Angela.
3. Expressed differently, there was a 99% certainty that the blood samples from the car came from the mother of Robbie and Angela.

The court affirmed the admission of a Cellmark generated RFLP test, under the *Frye* standard and affirmed the conviction of the defendant for murder. In a later case, *Missouri v. Davis*, 860 S.W.2d 369 (Mo. Ct. App. 1993), an intermediate Missouri appellate court affirmed the admission of DNA evidence without a *Frye* hearing. See also *Missouri v. Thomas*, 830 S.W.2d. 546 (Mo. Ct. App. 1992); *Missouri v. Hoff*, 1995 WL 396385 (Mo. Ct. App. July 6, 1995)(PCR).

§ 24 MONTANA:

In *Montana v. Moore*, 885 P.2d 457 (Montana Sup. Ct. 1994), the appellate court affirmed the defendant's conviction for murder and affirmed DNA testing using both the RFLP and PCR techniques which were performed on tissue found in the defendant's camper. The deceased's body was never found. In an interesting analysis, Cellmark Laboratories examined the DNA of the deceased's children and his mother and determined that the tissue found in the camper along with blood splattering belonged to the deceased. Five probes were used in the RFLP test; the PCR testing of the tissue was also admissible and any questions concerning contamination related to the weight of the evidence and not its admissibility.

In *Montana v. Weeks*, 891 P.2d 477 (Sup. Ct. 1995), the court affirmed the defendant's conviction for the rape of his twelve year old stepdaughter. She had given birth to his child. DNA RFLP testing by Genelex Corporation of the blood of the infant, the victim and the defendant indicated that the defendant was 154,000 times more likely to be the father than a random person, pursuant to a four probe match and a binning method similar to the FBI.

Serological ABO typing did not exclude the defendant and it was noted that he was 12.43 times more likely to be the father than a random Caucasian male. The Supreme Court also affirmed the use of DNA RFLP evidence and the statistical probabilities. *Accord, Missouri v. Hoff*, 1995 WL 396384 (Ct. App. July 6, 1995) (PCR); *Missouri v. Funke*, 1995 WL 418663 (Ct. App. July 18,1995).

§ 25 NEBRASKA:

In *Nebraska v. Houser*, 241 Neb. 525, 490 N.W.2d 168 (1992), the thirty-four year old victim was the girlfriend of the defendant. She was last seen driving to the defendant's home. Several hours later, the defendant telephoned the victim's parents inquiring of her whereabouts. He informed the parents that their daughter was at his home earlier and left to go to the grocery store and had not returned. The next day, when the victim was not heard from, the parents called the police. The police discovered the victim's car about four blocks from the defendant's home. The victim's purse and shoes were in the car. A huge pool of blood, a large sheet of plastic and a bloody hammer were in the trunk. Pieces of underbrush were wedged in the grill and on the passenger side door.

The defendant's car and apartment were searched and no apparent signs of a struggle were noted. However, sections of the carpeting and pillows with unclear stains were seized.

Further investigation uncovered several witnesses who were approached by the defendant on the evening of the victim's disappearance, requesting help in removing a car, matching the description of the victim's, from a ditch in which it was stuck.

The deceased's decomposed mud-covered body was discovered two months later, without any bodily fluids. The cause of death was determined to be strangulation. However, she also suffered multiple head wounds inflicted with a blunt object.

Blood was extracted from the cushions and carpet removed from the defendant's home.

Because the body of the victim was so badly decomposed, DNA testing could not be performed to determine her genetic makeup. There was no bodily fluids available.

However, DNA testing of the blood in the deceased's car, the hammer and the cushions and carpet were conducted. DNA testing of the mother and father of the victim was also conducted. It was determined that the blood on the cushion, carpet, trunk and hammer was deposited by a child of the parents. The surviving children of the parents were tested and were excluded as donors.

Genetic Fingerprinting:

The court reversed the conviction on the grounds that:

> "the trial court erred in plunging into this extremely technical evidence for the first time in the jury's presence" (490 N.W.2d at 181).

The trial court also erred in admitting this evidence because the prosecution did not lay the proper foundation. Although a Lifecodes employee testified that Lifecodes has a protocol and that she followed it in testing this evidence, there was no evidence that the protocol followed was established *according* to principles generally accepted in the relevant scientific fields.

The court also opined that a database of 900 to 1600 for Blacks and 1500 to 2500 for Caucasians may be insufficient and directed a hearing on this issue. It stated:

> "[w]e conclude that although it appears that the results of the DNA profile test are generally accepted in the relevant scientific communities and that such tests are reliable if performed in conformity with appropriate laboratory protocols, the probative value of population genetics probability testimony, at this time, must also be considered"(*Id.* at 184).

The court specifically rejected the defense contention that no DNA evidence is admissible until all laboratories adopt unified standards.

In a case dealing with PCR, the court opined that the calculation of the statistical probability is an essential part of the process used in determining the significance of a DNA match and, therefore, the underlying method of arriving at the calculation must also meet the *Frye* test for admissibility. The court further concluded that evidence of a DNA match will not be admissible unless accompanied by the statistical probability evidence that has been calculated using a generally accepted method. *Nebraska v. Carter*, 524 N.W.2d 763, 246 Neb. 953, (December 2, 1994).

§ 26 NEW HAMPSHIRE:

In *New Hampshire v. Vandebogart*, 616 A.2d 483 (N. H. Sup. Ct. 1992), the state Supreme Court found an FBI generated RFLP test admissible under a *Frye* test which looks to:
1) general acceptance in the relevant scientific community of the scientific theory or principle and

2) general acceptance in the relevant scientific community of the techniques, experiments or procedures applying that theory or principle.

The court held that the third prong of the *Castro* test goes to the weight of the evidence. It also found that RFLP analysis is generally accepted, and that whether the FBI used the proper matching window, lacked objective criteria for determining a match or whether the sample suffered from environmental insult were all questions of fact for the jury.

However, the court held that the FBI's statistical estimates are not generally accepted because of the population substructure controversy. The court indicated that the ceiling principle may solve this problem over the short-term and remanded for a hearing on that subject.

Upon rehearing, the appellate court affirmed the trial court's finding that the "ceiling principle" of calculating statistical probabilities met general acceptance in the relevant scientific community and courts may now take judicial notice of this finding. Further, the FBI method of calculating frequencies, which was admitted into evidence, although different from the "ceiling principle," was harmless error. *New Hampshire v. Vandebogart*, 652 A.2d 671 (N.H. Sup.Ct. January 19, 1995).

§ 27 NEW JERSEY:

In *New Jersey v. Williams*, 252 N.J. Super 369, 599 A.2d 960 (1991) (PCR), the court found that a Cetus generated PCR test (which examines the HLA DQ alpha portion of the genome) was admissible under a modified *Frye* standard which looks to the reliability of the evidence as well as the scientific consensus supporting it. *New Jersey v. Cary*, 49 N.J. 343, 230 A.2d 384 (1967); *Romano v. Kimmelman*, 96 N.J.66, 474 A.2d 1 (1984). That court also admitted a Gm/Km (Gamma marker/Kappa marker) test. In conjunction with the PCR results, the court allowed a product rule estimate based on all three tests that indicated that the blood in question is found in 1 out of every 800 Caucasians, and that 1,250,000 Caucasians on the planet could have these genetic characteristics. See also *New Jersey v. Thomas*, 245 N.J. Super. 428, 586 A.2d 250 (1991); *New Jersey v. Johnson*, N.Y. Times, January 31, 1995, p. B5, col. 1; *New Jersey v. Demarco*, 646 A.2d. 431 (N.J. Super. Ct. 1994).

§ 28 NEW MEXICO:

In *New Mexico v. Anderson*, 853 P.2d 135 (N.M. Ct. App. 1993), the victim met the defendant when she stopped at a convenience store to report her lost or stolen wallet. The defendant offered to loan her $10 if she would drive him home. The store clerk witnessed this interplay. The victim agreed. The defendant directed her to a field by his trailer home, where he proceeded to force her to perform oral sex. He ejaculated and forced her to swallow his semen. After complying, she vomited. The defendant severely beat the woman with a block of wood, causing injuries to her head which required 200 stitches.

The defendant was arrested after the victim identified him. Semen was recovered from the vomit. Upon arrest, the defendant was wearing a blood stained jacket. DNA testing of the semen matched the defendant's DNA profile. The jacket blood was matched to the DNA profile of the victim. The trial court admitted the DNA evidence including the statistical probabilities of 1 in 6.2 million for the sperm and 1 in 30 million for the jacket blood.

The Court of Appeals employed a *Frye* standard, and on authority of *New Mexico v. Lindemuth*, 243 P.2d 325 (N.M. Sup.Ct. 1952) (holding that it is best to err on the side of inadmissibility of novel evidence), the court rejected the FBI generated RFLP test on the grounds that the statistical calculations were not generally accepted. The court recognized that the clear weight of country-wide authority supports the admission of DNA evidence, but it reasoned that non-FBI cases and non-*Frye* cases are inapplicable, and thus reduced the precedent it would consider to five cases involving the FBI: *United States v. Two Bulls*, 918 F.2d 56 (8th Cir. 1990); *Hawaii v. Montalbo*, 828 P.2d 1274 (Hawaii Sup.Ct. 1992); *United States v. Yee*, 134 FRD 161, 181 (N.D. Ohio 1991); *People v. Mohit*, 153 Misc.2d 22 (West. Co. Ct. 1992); and *Massachusetts v. Lanigan*, 413 Mass. 154, 596 N.E.2d 311 (1992).

On the basis of this limited authority, the court held that the FBI's database and binning methodology had not been proven to be generally accepted among respected scientists and it reversed the trial court's order admitting the DNA evidence.

On appeal, the Supreme Court reversed the Court of Appeals refusal to admit DNA evidence and ruled that the statistical methodology employed by the testing laboratory was admissible. *New Mexico v. Anderson*, 115 N.M. 433, 881 P.2d 29 (1994). They affirmed the defendant's conviction of rape. *Accord, New Mexico v. Duran*, 81 P.2d 48 (N.M. Sup. Ct. 1994).

§ 29(a) NEW YORK STATE CASES
ADMITTING DNA IDENTIFICATION EVIDENCE:

People v. Wesley, 83 N.Y.2d 417 (1994) *aff'g*, 183 A.D.2d 75 (3d Dept. 1992) *aff'g*, 140 Misc.2d 306 (Alb. Co. Ct. 1988) (Harris, J.), approved the use of DNA (RFLP) evidence. The Court of Appeals found that the Lifecodes RFLP analysis in this case passed muster under the *Frye* analysis. It also affirmed the admission of Lifecodes' statistical estimate that the odds that the match between the decedent's blood and the blood stains on the clothes found in the defendant's apartment could have occurred randomly were 1 in 140 million. Lifecodes' determination that the defendant's blood was not the source of the stains on his clothing was also affirmed. The Court noted that these issues go to weight and not admissibility.

That court concluded that Lifecodes' protocols and scientific techniques are sufficiently established within the relevant scientific community to be accepted as reliable evidence and ruled that:

> "ancillary issues regarding integrity of the particular forensic sample from which the DNA fingerprint was obtained and whether the laboratory followed the accepted procedures in carrying out the tests on the particular sample at issue speak to the weight the evidence is *accorded* and thus are not relevant to the initial determination of admissibility."

People v. Wesley, supra, at 77-78. *Accord, People v. Moore,* 194 A.D.2d 32, 604 N.Y.S.2d 976 (3d Dept. 1993). The Court specifically made a distinction between the *Frye* issue and the foundation required for admission of evidence. The Court noted:

> "The focus moves from the general reliability concerns of *Frye* to the specific reliability of the procedures followed to generate the evidence proffered and whether they establish a foundation for the reception of the evidence at trial. The trial court determines, as a preliminary matter of law, whether an adequate foundation for the admissibility of this particular evidence has been established."

In *People v. Golub,* 196 A.D.2d 637 (1993), the Appellate Division, Second Department, also concluded that Lifecodes generated RFLP evidence should be admitted. The court found that there is no serious dispute in the legal or scientific communities that the process used to generate DNA identification evidence is valid and accepted in the scientific community. In *Golub,* the court noted that Lifecodes corrected the statistical errors noted in *Castro* and permitted Lifecodes statistical estimates of one in 250 million to one in 2 trillion. That court has also affirmed the conviction in another case in which DNA evidence was admitted. See *People v. Loliscio,* 187 A.D.2d 172

(2nd Dept. 1993), affirming *People v. Loliscio*, ___ Misc.2d ___ (Suff. Co. Ct., N.Y.L.J. September 12, 1990, Pg. 26 Col. 1), which admitted an FBI generated RFLP test and praised the FBI for its conservative statistical approach (1 in 25 million).

With four exceptions, the lower courts in New York State have also found this type of evidence admissible. In *People v. Mohit*, 153 Misc.2d 22 (West. Co. Ct. 1992) (Silverman, J.), the court found that an FBI generated RFLP test was admissible but concluded that the statistical estimate of the likelihood of a random match should be reduced to one in 100,000, the most conservative number possible. The circumstances of that case were highly unusual. The defendant, a physician, was accused of raping a patient. Semen recovered from the complainant was examined and matched the defendant's DNA profile. Nonetheless, the defendant denied sexual contact with the patient. The defendant was an Iranian Shiite Muslim and hailed from the town of Shustar where people frequently inter-marry at the level of first cousins for religious reasons. The defendant's family had done so for five generations. The court reasoned that, because of the long history of non-random mating in the defendant's family, the assumption of random mating, which underlies and validates the Hardy-Weinberg equation, could not be employed. Thus, the product rule calculation, which relies on the Hardy-Weinberg principle for its validity, was inadmissible.

With the estimate of a random match reduced to 1 in 100,000, the court permitted the evidence of the match to be considered by the jury. The jury evidently rejected the DNA evidence and found the defendant not guilty.

In *People v. Shi Fu Huang*, 145 Misc.2d 513 (Nass. Co. Ct. 1989), the court admitted a Lifecodes generated RFLP test, despite evidence of degradation in the forensic sample. Because Lifecodes' database contained only 167 samples of ethnic Chinese blood and Dr. Baird testified that 200 are needed for a valid statistical analysis of an ethnic group, however, the court concluded that it should reduce the estimate of the likelihood of a non-random match from 1 in 20 billion to 1 in 1 billion, the lowest figure agreed to by Dr. Baird. It submitted the question of the deficiency of the database and its effect on the reliability of Dr. Baird's estimate to the jury.

In *People v. Dabbs*, 154 Misc.2d 671 (Sup. Ct. West. Co. 1991), the court admitted a Lifecodes generated RFLP test excluding the defendant as the rapist and granted the defendant's application, pursuant to C.P.L. Art. 440, to vacate his conviction on the basis of this evidence. Notably, the People did not oppose the defendant's application. *People v. Dabbs, supra*, at 675. See also, *Matter of Washpon*,___ Misc.2d ___ (Sup. Ct. N.Y. Co., N.Y.L.J, March 27, 1995, Pg. 30, Col. 6). But see *People v. Brown*, 162 Misc.2d 555 (Cayuga Co. Ct. 1994) (The 440 application was denied on the grounds that the defendant had a copy of the blood sample and could have conducted its own testing, but failed to do so. The court thus distinguished *Dabbs*).

See also: *People v. Rivera*, ___ Misc.2d ___ (Suff. Co. Ct., N.Y.L.J. June 19, 1992, Pg. 26, Col. 1) (finding that an FBI generated RFLP test is admissible and its use of the product rule scientifically acceptable); *People v. Bertha L. English*, ___ Misc.2d ___ (Erie Co. Ct. Ind. No. 91-0694-001, Decided Oct. 27, 1992) (N.O.R.)* (Admitting a Lifecodes generated RFLP test, and, employing the ceiling principle[63], an estimate of the likelihood of a random match of 1 in 18,000; *affirmed*, 1995 WL 678268 (App. Div. 4th Dept., November, 15, 1995); (DNA identification is reliable, the RFLP technique is reliable and valid, and the Lifecodes' methodology in this case was reliable and yielded reliable results; deviations from the protocol and allegedly inconsistent or sloppy results go to the weight of the evidence); *People v. Rory Dolan*, ___ Misc.2d ___ (Suffolk Co. Ct. Case No. 0697-91, 1002-91,1556B-91, 0890-92, Decided April 4, 1993) (N.O.R.) (Admitting both an FBI generated RFLP test and Center for Blood Research (CBR) generated PCR test, and an estimate of 1 in 2½ million for a random match under the ceiling principle, which, the court found, is generally accepted for the purposes of forensic testimony. With regard to PCR, the court found that the DQ-Alpha test was generally accepted but that the DR-Beta test was not admissible as no database for this test was established. Questions regarding the integrity of the samples and the calculation as to the percent of the population go to the weight of the evidence and may be arguedto the jury); *People v. Gonzalez*, ___ Misc.2d ___ (Suff. Co. Ct., N.Y.L.J. August 8, 1989, Pg. 22, Col. 2) (Despite the fact defendant had already pleaded guilty, court discussed the DNA issue based on evidence adduced at a *Frye* hearing, and concluded that Lifecodes' generated RFLP test and estimate of 1 in 106,400 for a random match among Hispanics is admissible); *People v. Lopez*, ___ Misc.2d ___ (Sup. Ct. Queens Co, N.Y.L.J. January 6, 1989, Pg. 29, Col. 1) (Admitting a Lifecodes' generated RFLP test after a *Frye* hearing); *People v. Beauzil*, ___ Misc.2d ___ (Sup. Ct. Queens Co., N.Y.L.J. July 9, 1993, Pg. 25, Col. 1) (Admitting Lifecodes generated test [apparently RFLP] without a *Frye* hearing on authority of *People v. Wesley, supra*, and *United States v. Jakobetz*, 955 F.2d 786 (2d Cir. 1992)).[64]

In *People v. Morales*, ___ Misc.2d ___, (Rockland Co. Ct., N.Y.L.J. October 26, 1994, Pg. 34, Col. 6), the trial court reviewed the PCR DQ-Alpha and Polymarker tests manufactured by Perkin Elmer which examined five additional loci and found that the tests met *Frye* and were properly performed. However, the frequency probability of 1 in 22,434 was reduced to 1 in 2,243

---

* N.O.R. means "Not Officially Reported."

---

in accordance with the "ceiling principle" suggested by the National Research Council's 1992 report.

In *People v. Palumbo*, 162 Misc.2d 650 (Sup. Ct. Kings Co. 1994), the trial court denied the defendant's motion for a *Frye* hearing in a PCR DQ-Alpha test relying on *People v. Wesley* and other out of state jurisdictions which found that PCR testing meets *Frye*. The defendant's motion to compel the People to preserve a portion of the DNA sample was denied as the sample was consumed in the testing. Further, the defendant's request for proficiency testing documents of the analyst was denied. See also, *People v. Chalmers*, (Sup. Ct. West. Co., N.Y.L.J., May 3, 1994, Pg. 37, Col. 1.)

In *People v. Giomundo*, 619 N.Y.S.2d 894 (3d Dept. 1994) the appellate court affirmed the defendant's conviction for Murder in the Second Degree, noting that the admission of DNA evidence was not error as a proper foundation was laid, citing *People v. Wesley, supra*.

In *People v. White*, 621 N.Y.S.2d 728 (App. Div. 3d Dept. 1995), the appellate court affirmed the defendant's conviction for Rape in the Third Degree, noting that there was sufficient evidence at both the *Frye* hearing and trial demonstrating that the procedures followed in the Cellmark generated RFLP test were proper and scientifically acceptable. *Accord, People v. Vann*, ___ App. Div2d.___, (3d Dep't. 1995) 1995 WL 328048; *People v. Coit*, 621 N.Y.S.2d. 1023 (App. Div.4th Dept. 1994); *People v. King*, 161 Misc.2d. 448 (West. Co. Ct. 1994)(Blood properly seized for one rape may be used for DNA analysis in second unrelated rape).

In *People v. Rush*, ___ Misc.2d___, N.Y.L.J., 6/20/95, Pg. 31, Col. 2, (Marrus, J.), the trial court held that DNA RFLP evidence is sufficient to establish the identity of the defendant and to support conviction, where the complainant was unable to identify the defendant on trial. There was a four probe FBI generated RFLP match with a probability calculations of 1 in 500 million that DNA profile in semen could belong to anyone other than the defendant.

In *People v. Ladson*, ___ Misc. 2d___, N.Y.L.J., 4/4/95, Pg. 27, Col. 2, (Andrias, J.), the court held, after a pre-trial hearing, that both RFLP and PCR DNA profiling met *Frye*. The court presents an excellent analysis of "band shifting" resulting from degradation of the victim's autopsy blood when compared to the victim's vaginal fluids. *See also, People v. Watson* ___ Misc. 2d___, N.Y.L.J., 10/4/95, Pg. 1, Col. 1.

§ 29(b) NEW YORK STATE CASES REFUSING TO ADMIT DNA IDENTIFICATION EVIDENCE ON FOUNDATIONAL GROUNDS

In *People v. Castro*, 144 Misc.2d 956 (Sup. Ct. Bronx Co. 1989), (Sheindlin, J.) the court proposed a three-prong approach in determining the admissibility of DNA identification evidence. The first two prongs were directed toward resolving the *Frye* issue and the third prong was suggested to resolve the question of whether the particular tests sought to be admitted were properly performed. The three prongs were described as follows:

(1) is there a theory, generally accepted in the scientific community, that concludes that DNA forensic testing can produce reliable results

(2) are there techniques or experiments that currently exist, which are generally accepted in the scientific community, that are capable of producing reliable results in DNA identification and

(3) did the testing laboratory perform the accepted scientific techniques in analyzing the forensic samples in this particular case (*Id*. at 959).

The court concluded that the Lifecodes' procedures employed in that case were reliable to prove an exclusion, and that, in general, Lifecodes procedures are reliable to prove a match. In the case of the test before it, however, the match between the decedent's blood and the blood on the defendant's watch was excluded because there were two extra bands at DXYS14 for which there was no scientific explanation. While the laboratory possessed the necessary expertise to account for the band if further testing was possible, in that case the forensic sample had been consumed by prior RFLP tests, and further testing was impossible.[65] The two-prong *Castro* analysis of *Frye* and the third prong foundational analysis have been accepted by several states and some federal courts.

In *People v. Keene*, 156 Misc.2d 108 (Sup. Ct. Queens Co. 1992), the court rejected a Lifecodes generated RFLP test due to band shift and that laboratory's failure to use a monomorphic probe closest to the diagnostic probe to account for it.

In *People v Glen Ireland*,___Misc.2d___ (Onondaga Co. Ct. Ind. No. 90-815-1, Index No. 89-1725, Decided May 11, 1993) (N.O.R.), the court refused to admit an FBI created RFLP test, finding that, although the DNA technology can produce reliable results and the FBI protocols are accepted by the relevant scientific community, here the FBI failed to meet the third prong of the *Castro* test (the People having conceded that the *Castro* test controlled). The evidence was precluded for reasons that had nothing to do with its intrinsic validity. Rather, because the FBI agent who testified had not actually conducted the tests at issue, the court found no evidence (other than the agent's conclusory testimony) that the FBI's protocols had been followed in the case before it. The court also rejected the evidence concerning the likelihood of a random match between the samples because the FBI had not employed the ceiling principle in its calculations.

Genetic Fingerprinting:

§ 29(c) NEW YORK STATE CASES DENYING ADMISSION
ON GROUNDS OF FRYE

In *People v. Anthony Burton*, ___ Misc.2d ___ (Co. Ct. Sullivan Co. Decided Oct. 14, 1992) (N.O.R.) in a written opinion denying a motion for reargument, the court found that a CBR generated PCR DQ-Alpha test is inadmissible, based on its reading of the NRC April 1992 report. Nonetheless it found that a DQ-Alpha test which was not subject to PCR amplification would be admissible.[66]

§ 29(d) NEW YORK STATE AND FOUNDATION HEARINGS

Some disagreement exists in New York as to whether a pretrial hearing should be conducted to determine the admissibility of RFLP generated identification evidence. In *People v. Wesley*, 183 A.D.2d 75 (3d Dept. 1992), the Appellate Division held that arguable inadequacies in a specific test should not bar admissibility. Rather, the court believed that issues of that nature should be admissible and they go to the weight of the evidence. In *People v. Castro*, 144 Misc.2d 956 (Sup. Ct. Bronx Co. 1989) and *People v. Mohit*, 153 Misc.2d 22 (Co. Ct. West. Co. 1992), the courts reasoned that a pre-trial hearing should be required to determine if the laboratory correctly performed the tests. In *People v. Wesley*, (*supra*, Section 29(a)) the Court of Appeals noted that a foundational hearing for scientific evidence has always been the rule whether the scientific evidence is novel or not. Judge Smith explained the purpose of this hearing as follows:

> "foundation concerns itself with the adequacy of the specific procedures used to generate the particular evidence to be admitted."

Even the concurring opinion noted:

> "while trial courts may now take judicial notice of the tests' reliability, the adequacy of the methods used to acquire and analyze samples must be resolved case by case."

In dealing with the issue of population genetics, which is the most controversial area, the court simply noted:

> "population genetic issues go to the weight of the evi-

> dence and not its admissibility...even if the defense demonstrates inadequacy of the population studies, it does not exclude the evidence...the defendant may argue the inadequacy before the jury."[67]

See, *People v. Palumbo*, (Sup. Ct. Kings Co., N.Y.L.J, April 14, 1995, Pg. 31, Col. 5.)[68]

At present, it appears that there is scientific agreement that the scientific theory underlying this type of evidence is valid and that the process used to generate this type of evidence is reliable.[69] The courts in other states that have ruled on the admissibility of DNA identification evidence agree, for the most part, with the *Wesley* analysis.

In *People v. Davis*, 196 A.D.2d 597 (2d Dept. 1993), in a Lifecodes generated RFLP test wherein the random statistical evidence was one in 10 million, the Appellate Division reversed the conviction on the grounds that the defendant was denied discovery concerning the population genetic numbers. See also, *People v. DaGata*,___ N.Y.2d ___ (N.Y.L.J., 6/9/95, Pg. 27, Col. 1)(Even though FBI DNA tests were inconclusive, defendant entitled to notes concerning the procedures used. Prosecution's failure to comply with defendant's repeated requests resulted in remittal for disclosure of material and possible CPL 330.30 motion.)

In *People v. Jardin*,___App. Div. 2d.___ (1st Dept. 1995), the court affirmed 154 Misc2d. 172 (1992) (Sheindlin, J), wherein the trial court denied a defense request for a hearing to determine if the People were negligent in collecting and preserving vaginal swabs. The court also affirmed the trial court's ruling prohibiting the cross examination of the People's experts regarding defendant's DNA RFLP testing in which the results were inconclusive, where both sides conceded that the tests were properly performed. Identity was not an issue in the case as the defendant testified to consensual intercourse, but there was no evidence of ejaculation. Further, the trial court's preclusion of the defendant's consent to undergo DNA testing was proper and not admissible as "consciousness of innocence."

§ 30 NORTH CAROLINA:

In *North Carolina v. Hill*, 449 S.E.2d 573 (N.C. Ct. App. 1994), involving a FBI generated RFLP DNA test, wherein there was a four probe match between the defendant's blood and the recovered sperm and two inconclusive tests, the appellate court affirmed the rape conviction. It further affirmed the use of expert testimony which opined that within a reasonable degree of scientific certainty, it was the defendant who left the sperm and the statistical probability that anyone else had left the sperm was one in 2.6 million. The court further noted that the FBI population database was sufficient to generate the statistic.

In *North Carolina v. Pennington*, 327 N.C. 89, 393 S.E.2d 847 (1990), the court found a Cellmark generated RFLP test to be admissible under the "sufficiently reliable" standard of *North Carolina v. Bullard*, 312 N.C. 129, 322 S.E.2d 370 (1984) (the reliability of the evidence, not popularity in the scientific community, should control admission). Since the prosecution's evidence in favor of admission was uncontradicted, however, the court cautioned:

> "[w]hile we hold that evidence of DNA profile testing is generally admissible and was admissible in the present case, this should not be interpreted to mean that DNA test results should always be admitted into evidence."(393 S.E.2d at 854).

See *North Carolina v. Daughtry*, 1995 WL 444437 (N.C. Sup.Ct. 1995); *North Carolina v. Hunt*, 1994 WL 780915 (N.C. Sup.Ct. 1994); *North Carolina v. Futrell*, 112 N.C.App. 651, 436 S.E.2d 884 (1993); *North Carolina v. Bruno*, 424 S.E.2d 440 (N.C. Ct. App. 1993).

§ 31 OHIO:

In *Ohio v. Kinley*, 72 Ohio St.3d 491, 651 N.E.2d 419 (1995), a mother and her young son were found hacked to death. The defendant was seen in the area shortly before the murders. A machete was recovered behind his trailer home, and was subsequently linked by expert witnesses to the wounds on the deceased. A bloody jacket was recovered from the defendant. Blood was on the steering wheel of his car and bloody footprints, matching the defendant's size 10 shoes, were observed at the scene. The defendant admitted the killing to a friend, telling him that he "fucked them up." DNA testing of the jacket blood matched the DNA profile of one of the victims. The defendant was convicted of murder and sentenced to death. The Supreme Court affirmed the conviction and death sentence. The court ruled that the RFLP DNA tests were admissible. *Accord, Ohio v. Honzu*, 1995 WL 326214 (Ct. App. June 1, 1995)(PCR).

In *Ohio v. Pierce*, 64 Ohio St.3d 490, 597 N.E.2d 107 (1992), the court found admissible a Cellmark generated test and its statistical estimate of a random match of 1 in 40 billion under the relevance test of *Ohio Evid. R. #402, 403, 702* and *Ohio v. Williams*, 4 Ohio St.3d 53, 446 N.E.2d 444 (1983).

No pre-trial hearing is required in Ohio. Questions regarding the reliability and statistical estimates go to the weight of the evidence. *Accord*: *Ohio v. Thomas*, 63 Ohio App.3d 501, 579 N.E. 290 (1991) (Admitting a Cellmark generated RFLP test, under Ohio Evid. R.402, 403, 702). See *Ohio v. Nicholas*, 66 Ohio St. 3d 431, 613 N.E.2d 225 (1993); *Ohio v. Penton*, 1993 WL 102507 (Ohio Ct. App. April 7, 1993).

§ 32 OKLAHOMA:

In *Mitchell v. Oklahoma*, 884 P.2d 1186 (Okla. Crim. App. Ct. 1994), because a *Frye* hearing was not conducted due to the defense's failure to request one, the admission of DNA evidence was not error. The court noted, however, that in the appropriate case, it will decide whether to continue the *Frye* standard or adopt the standard set forth in *Daubert*. *See also, Taylor v. Oklahoma*, 889 P.2d. 319 (Ok. Crim. App. Ct. 1995).

§ 33 OREGON:

In *Oregon v. Futch*, 860 P.2d 264 (Or. Ct. App. 1993), the court ruled that a Lifecodes generated RFLP test was admissible under the guidelines found in *Oregon v. Brown*, 297 Or 404, 687 P.2d 751 (1984) and *Oregon Evidence Code Rules 401, 403, 702*, finding:

(1) that forensic DNA testing in general has sufficient scientific reliability so as to have probative value and can be helpful to the trier of fact in determining issues of identification
(2) that the probative value of this evidence outweighs its prejudicial effect (i.e. to overwhelm the jury) because the evidence is not infallible nor would it be considered as such by the fact finder, who will hear cross-examination and rebuttal testimony about the issue
(3) that following a battle of the experts at trial (nine experts for the state and six for the defense having testified) it could not be said that the state's evidence, concerning the testing procedures used in this case, was so lacking that it had no weight whatsoever.

It held that although reasonable fact-finders might differ as to whether the tests performed were accurate, it would be improper to pre-empt the jury's determination of that issue on the record. The court also approved of the use of a monomorphic probe to detect "bandshift." The disagreement in the statistical estimates about the likelihood of a random match, ranging from 1 in 66 billion to 1 in 130,000, was a question of fact for the jury. See *Oregon v. Herzog*, 125 Or. App. 10, 864 P.2d 1362 (1993); *Oregon v. Lyons*, 124 Or. App. 598, 863 P.2d 1303 (1993).

§ 34 PENNSYLVANIA:

In *Pennsylvania v. Rodgers*, 413 Pa Super 498, 605 A.2d 1228 (1992), the court admitted a Lifecodes generated RFLP test under the *Frye* standard. It found that once the evidence is ruled admissible, the question of whether the test was performed properly was for the jury to resolve. Since an expert testified for the defense and was given adequate opportunity to discredit the specific test results (although the defense expert testified that he was "very impressed" with the vast bulk of Lifecode's data and their autorads were "beautiful"), the jury had an adequate basis upon which to make its credibility determination. (605 A.2d at 1237). *Accord Pennsylvania v. Crews*, 640 A.2d 395 (Pa. Sup. Ct. 1994). *See also, Pennsylvania v. Francis*, 648 A.2d 49 (Pa. Super. Ct. 1994)(PCR); *Pennsylvania v. Brison*, 618 A.2d 420 (Pa. Super. Ct. 1992).

§ 35 SOUTH CAROLINA:

In *South Carolina v. Ford*, 392 S.E.2d 781 (S.C. Sup.Ct. 1990), the court admitted a Lifecodes generated RFLP test and its statistical estimate that the likelihood of a random match was 1 in 23 million, under both the *Frye* standard and the less restrictive standard of *South Carolina v. Jones*, 273 S.C.723, 259 S.E.2d 120 (1979). It held that future *Frye* hearings will not be required. The court further noted that:

> "DNA analysis may be admitted in judicial proceedings
> in this state in the same manner as other scientific evi-
> dence which is routinely used in trial court proceedings
> such as fingerprint analysis and ABO blood tests."

(392 S.E.2d at 784). However, the admissibility of this evidence in South Carolina courts remains subject to an attack on the reliability of the specific test at issue, or an attack on the chain of evidence.

> "The evidence may be found to be so tainted that it is
> totally unreliable and, therefore, must be excluded." (*id* at 784.)

Accord: South Carolina v. Dinkins, 1995 WL 447513 (S.C. Ct. App. 1995); *South Carolina v. McFadden*, 1995 WL 235041 (S.C. Ct. App. 1995); *South Carolina v.*

China, 440 S.E.2d 382 (S.C. Ct. App. 1993).

§ 36 SOUTH DAKOTA:

In *South Dakota v. Wimberly*, 467 N.W.2d 499 (S.D. Sup.Ct. 1991), the court held that FBI generated RFLP DNA analysis meets the *Frye* standard based on uncontradicted testimony. It stated however, that

> "[w]e affirm the trial court on this issue, but caution that
> our holding does not 'rubber stamp' as admissible DNA
> test results in all cases." (*id* at 506.)

An attack on the reliability of the specific test remains and evidence may be found to be so unreliable that it must be excluded.
Accord, South Dakota v. Schweitzer, 533 N.W.2d 156 (S.D. Sup. Ct. 1995) (PCR & statistics of 1 in 18,300).

§ 37 TENNESSEE:

In *King v. Tennessee*, No. 01C01-9310-CR-00366, 1994 WL 406173 (unpublished) (Tenn. Crim. App. August 4, 1994), the appellate court affirmed the defendant's conviction for rape noting that *Tennessee Code Ann. 24-7-117* permits DNA to be admissible in evidence without a preliminary hearing. The court further approved the testimony of the FBI expert that the FBI generated RFLP DNA testing excluded 99.9999% of the population as possible sources of the stains.

§ 38 TEXAS:

In *Brown v. Texas*, 881 S.W.2d 582 (Tex. Ct. App. 1994), the court affirmed a conviction for Rape in the First Degree. It noted that an FBI generated RFLP test (where there was a three probe match and one inconclusive test) and the expert opinion giving a probability of 1 in 200,000 were reliable and admissible. It also noted that ABO and PGM tests did not exclude the defendant. Further, this 1994 decision approved the FBI method of "binning" to calculate the probabilities. Also of interest is the court's approval of the use of the prosecution's expert witness to render two opinions:

(1) the DNA testing demonstrates an "extremely strong or powerful association between the defendant and the recovered semen"

(2) the "likelihood of the disputed sperm coming from some-

one else is very small." *Brown v. Texas, supra* at p. 585.

In *Turner v. Texas*, 886 S.W.2d 859 (Tex. Ct. App. 1994), the appellate court affirmed the defendant's conviction for murder and the use of DNA evidence and statistical probabilities in a state crime lab generated RFLP test. *Accord, Campbell v. Texas*, 1995 WL 354071, (Decided June 14, 1995), the Texas Court of Criminal Appeals affirmed the death penalty imposed upon the defendant's conviction for rape and murder. PCR testing was conducted by Serological Research Institute located in California and found admissible.

In the earlier case of *Mandujano v. Texas*, 799 S.W.2d 318 (Tex. Ct. App. 1990), the court found a Lifecodes generated RFLP test and that laboratory's statistical estimate of a random match of 1 in 2.4 billion admissible under what appears to be the *Frye* standard. However, in *Glover v. Texas*, 825 S.W.2d 127 (Tex. Crim. App. 1992), the Court of Criminal Appeals held that *Rule 702* of the *Texas Rules of Criminal Evidence* governs the admission of all novel scientific evidence and, under that standard, the court determined that a DNA RFLP test and statistical estimate of a random match of 1 in 18 billion was admissible. *See also: Vickers v. Texas*, 801 S.W.2d 214 (Tex. Ct. App. 1990) (No error in refusing to hold a pre-trial or mid-trial hearing on the admissibility of DNA identification evidence); *Barnes v. Texas*, 839 S.W.2d 118 (Tex. Ct. App. 1992). *See Flores v. Texas*, 871 S.W.2d 741 (Tex. Crim. App. 1993) *rehearing denied* March 9, 1994.

In *Kelly v. Texas*, 824 S.W.2d 568 (Tex. Crim. App. 1992) *(en banc)*, the court sanctioned a Lifecodes generated RFLP test and its statistical estimate of a random match of 1 in 13 million under a reliability test, derived from *Texas Rules of Criminal Evidence 702*, which requires a showing, by clear and convincing evidence, that:

(a) the underlying scientific theory is valid
(b) the technique applying the theory is valid, and
(c) the technique was properly applied on the occasion in question.
   (*id* at 573).

The Court of Criminal Appeals adhered to this ruling in *Glover v. Texas*, 825 S.W.2d 127 (Tex. Cr. App. 1992), holding that *Rule 702 of the Texas Rules of Criminal Evidence* governs the admission of all novel scientific evidence and, under that standard, that court found that a DNA RFLP test and statistical estimate of a random match of 1 in 18 billion was admissible.

In another case, *Bethune v. Texas*, 821 S.W.2d 222 (Tex. Ct. App. 1991), *aff'd* 828 S.W.2d 14 (Tex. Crim. App. 1992), the court admitted a Lifecodes generated RFLP test, based upon the record before it. The prosecution's single expert was uncontroverted.

In *Clarke v. Texas*, 813 S.W.2d 654 (Tex. App.—Fort Worth 1991), *aff'd* 839 S.W.2d 92 (Tex. Crim. App. 1992) evidence generated through an unnamed laboratory's PCR analysis, which examined the DQ-Alpha locus, was admitted under both the *Frye* standard and the relevancy standard of *Tex. R. Crim. Evid 401, 402, 702*. See *Hicks v. Texas*, 860 S.W.2d 419 (Tex. Crim. App. 1993); *Williams v. Texas*, 848 S.W.2d 915 (Tex. Ct. App. 1993); *Fuller v. Texas*, 827 S.W.2d 919 (Tex. Crim. App. 1992); *Trimboli v. Texas*, 826 S.W.2d 953 (Tex. Crim. App. 1992), *affirming* 817 S.W.2d 785 (Tex. Ct. App. 1991) (RFLP and PCR analysis performed); *McLaughlin v. Texas*, No. B14-91-00872-CR, 1993 WL 22050 unpublished (Tex. Ct. App. February 4, 1993) *affirming* No. B14-91-00872-CR, 1992 WL 370411 unpublished (Tex. Ct. App. Dec. 17, 1992); *Lopez v. Texas*, 793 S.W.2d 738 (Tex. Ct. App. 1990).

§ 39 VERMONT:

In *Vermont v. Passino*, 658 A. 2d. 38 (Vt. Sup. Ct. 1994), the Supreme Court reversed the defendant's conviction for manslaughter due to the trial court's prejudicial ruling precluding an FBI generated RFLP test excluding the defendant.

In *Vermont v. Streich*, 1995 WL 73724, decided February 17, 1995, the Supreme Court affirmed the admission of RFLP DNA evidence produced by the FBI. In thoroughly analyzing the problems surrounding statistical calculations, the court disapproved of the use of an "unmodified product rule" due to the controversy involving subpopulations. However, the court noted that they would approve statistical calculations which used a more conservative method of calculation. The Supreme Court also announced that Vermont will henceforth use the *Daubert* standard of admissibility in place of *Frye*.

§ 40 VIRGINIA:

In *Spencer v. Commonwealth*, 238 Va. 275, 384 S.E.2d 775, (1989), *cert.den.*, 493 U.S. 1036, 110 S.Ct. 759; 107 L.Ed 775 (1990) (*Spencer I*), a capital case, the court found admissible a Lifecodes generated RFLP test and Lifecodes' statistical estimate of a random match of 1 in 135 million (there being approximately 10 million adult Black males in the United States at the time) using a reliability test, upon the authority of *O'Dell v. Commonwealth*, 234 Va. 672, 695-96, 364 S.E.2d 491, 504 (Sup. Ct. 1988), but it noted (at n.10) that DNA evidence would pass muster under the *Frye* test as well. The defense had offered no evidence to counter that given by the prosecution, and, as a result, the court found that since the undisputed evidence supports the conclusion that both DNA analysis in general and the tests performed in this case were reliable, the trial court had not erred in admitting the evidence. *Accord Spencer v. Commonwealth*, 238 Va. 295, 384 S.E.2d 785 (1989), *cert. den.*, 493 U.S. 1093, 110 S.Ct. 1171, 107 L.Ed 1073 (1990) denial of Writ of Habeas Corpus affirmed, 18 F.3d. 237 (4th Cir. 1994) (*Spencer II*) (admitting DNA); *Spencer v. Commonwealth*, 238 Va. 563, 385 S.E.2d 850 (1989) *cert. den.* 493 U.S. 1093, 110 S.Ct. 1171, 107 L.Ed 1073 (1990) denial of Writ of Habeas Corpus affirmed, 18 F.3d. 229 (4th Cir. 1994) (*Spencer III*) (admitting DNA evidence for reasons stated in *Spencer I* and *Spencer II*) *Spencer v. Commonwealth*, 249 Va, 78, 393 S.E.2d 609 (1990), *cert. den.* 493 U.S. 1073, 110 S.Ct. 1171, 107 L.Ed 1073 (*Spencer IV*) (evidence of PCR generated DNA analysis admitted under relevancy test). See *Satcher v. Commonwealth*, 244 Va. 220, 421 S.E.2d 821 (1992). *Accord, Brown v. Commonwealth*, 1995 WL 378611 (Va. Ct. App. June 27, 1995)(PCR).

In *Husske v. Virginia*, 448 S.E.2d 331 (Va. Ct. App. 1994), the appellate court reversed the defendant's conviction on the grounds that the trial court committed error in not approving state funds for the defense to hire an expert to controvert the prosecution's DNA results. It otherwise affirmed the FBI generated RFLP testing and the 1 in 700,000 statistic obtained through the "binning" method.

§ 41 WASHINGTON:

In *Washington v. Russell*, 882 P.2d 747 (Wash. Sup. Ct. 1994) (PCR), the appellate court affirmed the defendant's conviction for rape wherein a part of the evidence was PCR (DQ Alpha) performed by Dr. Edward Blake of Forensic Science Associates. The court found that PCR (DQ Alpha) met *Frye* and noted that the defendant's attack claiming a high risk of contamination was speculative as the defense expert testified that he observed no contamination in the instant matter. The court further noted that the second defense expert, who opined that PCR is not presently sufficiently developed for use in criminal cases, is himself consistently using PCR in his laboratory. The court further approved the expert opinion that the defendant's DQ Alpha profile occurred in only five to ten percent of the population and allowed the opinion that ninety to ninety-five percent of the population may be excluded. Population figures were not otherwise offered.

In *Washington v. Buckner*, 876 P.2d 910 (Wash. Ct. App. 1994), the court affirmed the defendant's murder conviction. In this Lifecodes generated RFLP DNA test where there was a four probe match, the court allowed the expert to testify to a one in 19 billion calculation and also affirmed the use of the expert's opinion which stated:

> "There is no doubt in my mind that the sample came from the same person."

In a separate issue, the court ruled that it was not a violation of the defendant's rights for the prosecution to use as much of the sample as necessary even if it results in an insufficient sample to permit the defendant to independently perform DNA testing.

However, on appeal, the Supreme Court of Washington reversed Buckner's conviction on the grounds that the prosecution expert was permitted to testify that the defendant's matching DNA profile was "unique in the population." Cautioning that such language must be avoided, the court noted that the calculations producing figures of 1 in 19 billion were not performed in conformity with the ceiling principle, which, if used, would be acceptable (890 P2d. 460)(1995).

In *Washington v. Cauthron*, 120 Wash.2d 879, 846 P.2d 502 (1993), the facts indicated that between the years 1986 and 1987, a series of 20 to 25 rapes were committed under similar circumstances. The rapist, wearing a ski mask, cloth gloves and armed with a black pistol, would accost females in their car, blind fold them with their own clothes after stripping them naked and proceed to rape them. He then would force the victims to pose nude and take pictures of them. He threatened to show the photos if the victim told anyone about the crime. In 1988, a complaint was received of a man wearing a ski mask masturbating in some bushes. Upon arrival, the police observed the defendant in the bushes with his pants undone, exposing pubic hair and a part of his penis. Nearby was a ski mask, a pair of cloth gloves and a toy black pistol. DNA testing was conducted on the semen previously recovered and preserved from the crime scene and the clothing of five victims and compared with the defendant's DNA profile. There was a match on each of the items tested. None of the victims could identify the defendant on trial. Nonetheless, the defendant was found guilty of the rapes.

The court found that RFLP typing is universally accepted and therefore admissible under a *Frye* standard as set forth in *Washington v. Martin*, 101 Wash.2d 713, 684 P.2d 651 (1984).

The court, in dealing with the defendant's argument concerning potential problems, noted:

> "[c]ontamination of the sample, degradation due to the passage of time, and human error are [potential prob-

lems]... While these problems are of some concern, they do not require excluding the evidence altogether. Once the general underlying principles are accepted, as they are here, then both the proponent and opponents of a particular test should be able to garner the necessary information to present both sides of the issue to the factfinder...we hold that the problems raised by the defense concerning the quality of the autorads in this case go to the weight rather than the admissibility of the testimony"(846 P.2d at 511-12).

Nonetheless the court reversed the conviction because the trial court had permitted the Cellmark laboratory experts to testify that the DNA recovered from the victim "matched" the defendant's DNA without offering any testimony regarding linkage equilibrium or Hardy-Weinberg equilibrium or any probability statistics to support that assertion. The court stated that testimony regarding population statistics offered in conformity with the 1992 NRC report would be admissible in Washington.[70] *See, Washington v. Kalakosky*, 121 Wash.2d 525, 852 P.2d 1064 (1993). *See also, Washington v. Gentry*, 888 P.2d. 1105 (Wash. Sup. Ct. 1995).

§ 42 WEST VIRGINIA:

In *West Virginia v. Woodall*, 385 S.E.2d 253 (W.Va. Sup. Ct. App. 1989), in ruling on defendant's application to admit a Cellmark generated RFLP test, which found insufficient high molecular weight DNA in semen recovered from the complainant to produce an interpretable result, the court found that trial court's initial refusal to admit the test was harmless. With regard to DNA evidence in general, however, the court found that, under a combination of *Frye* and *W.Va. Rules of Evidence 403 and 707*, the DNA typing analysis was so generally accepted that, henceforth, it can be admitted by judicial notice. Future *Frye* hearings will not be required in West Virginia. In extreme cases, DNA evidence will be excluded if irrelevant or unreliable, but, otherwise, arguments regarding the reliability of a specific test go to the weight of the evidence.

§ 43 WYOMING:

In *Springfield v. Wyoming*, 860 P.2d 435 (Wyo. Sup. Ct. 1993), the highest court found that FBI generated RFLP test matching defendant to the forensic sample and excluding his brothers was admissible under *Wyo. Rule of*

Evidence 702 and *Rivera v. Wyoming*, 840 P.2d 933 (Wyo. Sup. Ct. 1992). The court further ruled that any concerns about the specific procedures employed go to the weight of the evidence, following *Illinois v. Lipscomb*, 215 Ill. App.3d 413, 574 N.E.2d 1345 (1991) and *United States v. Jakobetz*, 955 F.2d 786 (2d Cir. 1992). The court also found admissible an estimate of a random match of 1 in 17 million for blacks and 1 in 221,000 for Native Americans (defendant being 3/4 Native American from the Crow tribe and 1/4 Black despite the fact that no members of the Crow Nation were included in the Native American databank). The Court concluded that any question concerning the size of the database or Hardy-Weinberg equilibrium goes to the weight of the evidence and is properly left to the jury.

§ 44 THE FEDERAL COURTS:

In *United States v. Yee*, 129 F.R.D. 629 (N.D. Ohio 1990), 134 F.R.D. 161 (N.D. Ohio 1991), *aff'd* 12 F.3d 540 (6th Cir. 1993), the court admitted a FBI generated RFLP test and an estimate of the likelihood of a random match of 1 in 35,000, under the *Frye* standard. The court found that the general scientific community accepts the FBI's procedures and protocols despite the conflict between the defense and prosecution experts. The Sixth Circuit Court of Appeals in *United States v. Bonds*, 12 F.3d 540 (6th Cir. 1993) *affirming* 134 F.R.D. 161 (N.D. Ohio 1991) formerly reported as, and more widely known as, *United States v. Yee*) rendered a significant opinion in the area of population frequency data. The court recognized that between the hearing held by the magistrate and the current appeal, the Supreme Court decided *Daubert*. Nonetheless, the court concluded that the evidence introduced at the *Frye* hearing was clearly sufficient to justify admission under the new statndard announced in *Daubert*. This court made significant findings and observations. First, the court refused to consider the 1992 NRC report inasmuch as that report was unavailable at the time of the evidentiary hearing conducted two years prior to its release. The Court of Appeals concluded that to include the report in its determination would subvert the right of both parties to rebut the report's contents with proper testimony and other evidence before the trial court. Notwithstanding that refusal, the court noted the substance of the report regarding the question of population substructuring was presented by expert testimony in the trial court hearing, including that of Drs. Lewontin and Hartl. Specifically, the court determined:

> "Because the DNA results were based on scientifically
> valid principles derived from scientifically valid proce-

dures, it is not dispositive that there are scientists who vigorously argue that the probability estimates are not accurate or reliable because of the possibility of ethnic substructure. The potential of procedures used by the BI are not generally accepted; it means only that there is a dispute over whether the results are as accurate as they might be and what, if any, weight the jury shouldgive those results." (*id at* 564-565)

The court, using the standards set forth in *Daubert,* upheld the admissibility of the evidence. Additionally, the court noted that the evidence presented at the hearing permitted admission even under the *Frye* standard. The court reasoned:

"We note that because we have found that the FBI's DNA principles and procedures are generally accepted by the scientists in the field, the FBI's principles and procedures have met the standard the Supreme Court has labelled as 'rigid', 'at odds with the "liberal thrust" of the Federal Rules', 'austere' and 'uncompromising'. Daubert, 113 S.Ct. at 2794, 2798. Accordingly, it is difficult to see how the FBI's theory and procedures would not pass muster under the more 'liberal' Rule 702 analysis set out in Daubert. If under the 'rigid' general acceptance standard we would have affirmed the admissibility of the DNA testimony and evidence, we certainly have little problem upholding the admission under this more lenient 'scientific validity' test." (*id at* 566, fn. 21).

See also, Spencer v. Murray, 5 F.3d 758 (4th Cir. 1993) (death sentence appeal from state convictions). See *Spencer v. Commonwealth,* Section J&40, *supra.*

In *United States v. Jakobetz,* 955 F.2d 786 (2d Cir. 1992), *cert. den.,* 113 S.Ct. 104, 61 U.S.L.W. 3257 (U.S. 1992) *aff'g.* 747 F. Supp. 250 (D. Vt. 1990), the court found that an FBI generated RFLP test and a statistical estimate of the likelihood of a random match of 1 in 300 million was admissible under Fed. Rules of Evidence 403 and 702, which allows a more permissive standard than *Frye.*

The Second Circuit rejected the argument that the DNA test at issue must be demonstrated to be correctly performed and reliable in a pre-trial hearing before the jury hears the evidence, reasoning that although DNA evidence does present special challenges:

> "We do not think that they are so special as to require a
> new standard of admissibility. (*United States v. Williams,*
> 583 F.2d 1194, 1198 (2d.Cir. 1978)) *cert. den.* 439 U.S. 1117
> (1979) the *Williams* test is not a difficult hurdle that
> excludes highly relevant evidence simply because it is
> complicated. The focus of the court must be on 'the
> admissibility or non-admissibility of a particular type of
> scientific evidence', not the truth or falsity of an alleged
> scientific fact or truth. In other words, the court need not
> make the initial determination that the expert testimony
> or the evidence proffered is true before submitting the
> information to the jury. The court must allow the jury to
> discharge its duties of weighing the evidence, making
> credibility determinations, and ultimately deciding the
> facts."(*id* at 796-797).

That court ruled that a trial court may take judicial notice of the general acceptability of such evidence and the general theories and specific techniques involved in DNA profiling.

> "Beyond such judicial notice, the threshold for admissi-
> bility should require only a preliminary showing of reli-
> ability of the particular data to be offered i.e., some indi-
> cation of how the laboratory work was done and what
> analysis and assumptions underlie the probability calcu-
> lations." (*id* at 799-800).

In *United States v. Martinez,* 3 F.3d 1191 (8th Cir. 1993),[71] the Court of Appeals for the Eighth Circuit found that a FBI generated RFLP test was admissible under the standard announced in *Daubert v. Merrill Dow Pharmaceuticals,* Inc., 113 S. Ct. 2786 (Decided June 28, 1993). That court agreed with the Second Circuit that the general theory and techniques of DNA profiling are valid and that in the future courts may take judicial notice of their reliability. However, new techniques are offered the courts will be required to hold a hearing under the *Daubert* standard.

The fact that judicial notice may be taken, the court ruled, does not mean that expert testimony concerning DNA profiling is automatically admissible under *Daubert.*[72] The court should make an initial inquiry into the particular expert's application of the scientific principle or methodology. The trial court should require the testifying expert to provide evidence by affidavit attesting that he or she properly performed the protocols involved in DNA profiling.

Genetic Fingerprinting:

Upon challenge to the application of the protocols by the opponent, the court must determine whether the expert erred in applying the protocols, and if so, whether such error so infected the procedure as to make the results unreliable. *Accord, United States v. Johnson*, 56 F.3d 947 (8th Cir. 1995).

No federal court has outright rejected DNA identification evidence. However, two courts have made preliminary determinations that a given test would not be admitted as presently presented.

In *United States v. Two Bulls*, 918 F.2d 56 (8th Cir. 1990), vacated and indictment dismissed after remand by reason of defendant's death, 925 F.2d 1127 (8th Cir. 1990), the court below had ruled admissible an FBI generated RFLP test under Fed. Rule of Evidence 702. The Eighth Circuit vacated that ruling and remanded for an expanded hearing, finding that Rule 702 does not supersede *Frye*. The court directed that the three prong *Castro* test is to be adopted at the hearing.

> "The trial court is to decide (1) whether DNA evidence is generally accepted by the scientific community, (2) whether the testing procedures used in this case are generally accepted as reliable if performed properly, (3) whether the test was properly performed in this case, (4) whether the evidence is more prejudicial than probative in this case, and (5) whether the statistics used to determine the probability of someone else having the same genetic characteristics is more probative than prejudicial under Rule 403." (*id at* 61.)

In *United States v. Young*, 754 F.Supp. 739 (D.So.Dakota 1990), a 15 year old was the victim of a rape and impregnated. She named the defendant as her attacker. She underwent an abortion and the aborted fetus was subjected to DNA analysis. Upon analysis of the defendant's DNA profile, the results established that he was the father of the aborted fetus. The court applied the standard of *United States v. Two Bulls, supra*, and admitted a Cellmark generated RFLP test under *Fed. Rule of Evidence 403*. The court made no specific ruling on the admissibility of the statistical evidence since defendant withdrew his objection to the statistical estimate. Thus, evidence that the chance of a random match was 1 in 4 million was admissible at trial. *Accord, United States v. Chischilly*, 30 F.3d 1144 (9th Cir. 1994).

In *United States v. Davis and Reed*, 40 F.3d 1069 (10th Cir. 1994), the Tenth Circuit Court of Appeals affirmed the murder convictions of the defendants. It noted that a FBI generated RFLP test wherein the DNA sample was recovered from the bone chip found in a car matched the defendant Davis' DNA and that blood on recovered clothing matched defendant *Reed*'s DNA. Population frequencies of 1 in 30,000 for Davis and 1 in 600,000 for *Reed* were found to be admissible. The court noted:

> "Statistical probabilities are basic to DNA analysis and their use has been widely researched and discussed... The district court did not abuse its discretion by finding that the statistical evidence was more probative than prejudicial."

It is noted that the court evaluated DNA forensic evidence using *Daubert* guidelines but found that under either the *Frye* or the *Daubert* standard the DNA evidence was admissible.

For an interesting analysis of RFLP, PCR and AMPFLP DNA testing by a German laboratory, see *United States v. Thomas*, 1995 WL 565101 (U.S. Air Force Ct. Crim. App. September 12, 1995).

SECTION K

STATE STATUTES ADMITTING DNA IDENTIFICATION EVIDENCE IN CRIMINAL PROCEEDINGS

1. **Alabama:** Code of Alabama 36-18-30 (1994)
2. **Alaska:** Alaska Stat. 12.45 (1995)
3. **Connecticut:** 1994 Conn. Legis. 94-246 (SHB 5789) (1994)
4. **Delaware:** Del. Code Ann. tit. 29, 3512 (1994)
5. **Indiana:** Ind. Code Ann. 35-37-5-13 (West 1993)
6. **Louisiana:** La. Rev. Stat. Ann. 15:441.1 (West 1992)
7. **Maryland:** Md. Code Ann., Cts. & Jud. Proc. 10-915 (Michie 1992)
8. **Minnesota:** Minn. Stat. Ann. 634.25, 634.26 (West 1992)
9. **Nevada:** Nev. Rev. Stat. 56.020 (Supp. 1989)
10. **North Dakota:** N.D. Cent. Code 31-13-01 et. seq. (1995)
11. **Oklahoma:** Okla. Stat. Ann. tit. 22, 751.1 (West 1992)
12. **Tennessee:** Tenn. Code Ann. 24-7-117 (1992)
13. **Virginia:** Va. Code Ann. 19.2-270.5 (Michie 1992)
14. **Wisconsin:** Wisc. Stat. Ann. 972.11(5) (1993)

SECTION L

STATE LEGISLATION CREATING DNA DATABANKS FOR USE IN CRIMINAL INVESTIGATIONS

1. **Alabama:** Code of Alabama 36-18-20 et. seq. (1994)
2. **Alaska:** Alaska Stat. 22.20 & 44.41.035 (1995)
3. **Arizona:** Ariz. Rev. Stat. Ann. 31-281 (1992)
4. **Arkansas:** House Bill No. 1560 (April 5, 1995)
5. **California:** Cal. Penal Code 290.2 (West 1992)
6. **Connecticut:** 1994 Conn. Legis. 94-246 (S.H.B. 5789)(1994)
7. **Colorado:** Colo. Rev. Stat. 17-2-201 (1993)
8. **Delaware:** Del. Code Ann. tit. 29, 4713 (1994)
9. **Florida:** Fla. Stat. Ann. 943.325 (West 1992)
10. **Georgia:** Ga. Code Ann. 24-4-60, 24-4-64 (1992)
11. **Hawaii:** Haw. Rev. Stat. 706-603 (1992)
12. **Illinois:** Ill. Rev. Stat. ch. 730, 5/5-4-3 (1992)
13. **Indiana:** Ind. Code 20-12-34.5 et. seq. (1990)
14. **Iowa:** Iowa Code Ann. 13.10, 901.2, 906.4 (West 1992)
15. **Kansas:** 1991 Kans. Sess. Laws Ch. 92 (1991) (*see, Vanderlinden v. Kansas*, 874 F. Supp. 1210 (D. Kansas 1995) (State statute requiring inmate's blood for DNA database constitutional).)
16. **Kentucky:** Ky. Rev. Stat. Ann. 17.170 (Michie/Bobbs- Merrill 1992)
17. **Louisiana:** La. Rev. Stat. Ann. 15-535, 15-578 (West 1992)
18. **Maine:** Me. Rev. Stat. Ann. Tit. 25, 1531 et. seq. (1995)
19. **Maryland:** 1994 Maryland Laws Ch. 458 (H.B. 410) (1994)
20. **Michigan:** Mich. Comp. Laws 750.520m (1992)
21. **Minnesota:** Minn. Stat. Ann. 299C.155, 609.3461 (1993)
22. **Mississippi:** Senate Bill No. 2482 (commencing January 6, 1996)
23. **Missouri:** Mo. Ann. Stat. 650.050, 650.053, 650.055, 650.057 (Vernon 1992)
24. **Montana:** Mont. Code Ann. 41-5-604 (1995)
25. **Nevada:** Nev. Rev. Stat. 176.111 (Michie 1991)
26. **New Jersey:** N.J. Stat. Ann. 53:1:20.17 et. seq. (1995)
27. **New York:** CPL 165.10 et. seq., Exec. Law 837 et. seq., PL 240. 70 et. seq. (July 1994)
28. **North Carolina:** N.C. Gen. Stat. 15A-266.1 et. seq. (1993)
29. **North Dakota:** N.D. Cent. Code 31-13-01 et. seq. (1995)
30. **Ohio:** Ohio Rev. Code 2901.07 (May 31, 1995)
31. **Oklahoma:** Okla. Stat. Ann. tit. 57, 584 (1991); Okla. Stat. Ann. tit. 74, 150.2, 150.27, 150.28 (1993)
32. **Oregon:** Or. Rev. Stat. 181.085 (1991)
33. **Pennsylvania:** Penn. Con. Stat., Title 18, S 9209 (1995)

34. **South Carolina:** S.C. Gen. Stat. 15A-266.1 et. seq. (1993)
35. **South Dakota:** S.D. Codified Laws Ann. 23-5-14, 23-5-15, 32-5-17 (1992)
36. **Tennessee:** Tenn. Code Ann. 38-6-113, 40-35-321 (1992)
37. **Texas:** Tex. Code Ann. 411.141 et. seq. (1995)
38. **Utah:** Utah Code Ann. 1953 53.5-212.1 et. seq. (1994)
39. **Virginia:** Va. Code Ann. 2.1-434.1; 19.2-310.2; 19.2-310.3; 19.2-310.7; 19.2-387 (Michie 1992)
40. **Washington:** Wash. Rev. Code Ann. 43.43.752; 43.43.754; 43.43.756; 43.43.758 (West 1992)
41. **West Virginia:** West Va. Code 15-2-24a (1993)
42. **Wisconsin:** Wisc. Stat. Ann. 973.047, 165.76, 165.77

Genetic Fingerprinting:

GLOSSARY OF TERMS COMMONLY USED
IN DNA FORENSIC ANALYSIS

A

Adenine	One of the four bases found in the DNA helix; will only combine with thymine. See also, cytosine, guanine and thymine.
Agarose Gel	A gelatin-like substance into which DNA is loaded for electrophoresis.
Aliquoted lots, probes or batches.	Measured amounts of materials taken from original lots, probes or batches.
Allele	One specific form of a given gene.
Anneal	Pairing complimentary strands of DNA to form double helix.
Anonymous Loci	Specific sites on chromosome where the gene functions have not been identified.
ASCLD	American Society of Crime Laboratory Directors.
Autorad	An x-ray film of the hybridization between the radioactive probe and the complementary exposed strand of DNA.
Autorads—Blue	Copies of autorads made from the original grey autorads.
Autorads—Grey	Original autorads.
Autoradiography	The process of making an autorad.
Autosomes	The forty-four chromosomes (excluding the X and Y sex chromosomes) found in human cells.

B

Bacterial DNA	The DNA found in bacteria.
Band	A radioactive signal on an autorad usually caused by a fragment of human or bacterial DNA.
Band Shifting	Bands which visually do not appear to co-migrate, but can be declared a match because of gel shift.
Base Pair	The combination of either adenine and thymine, or cytosine and guanine. Base pairs form the rungs of the DNA helix (spiral ladder).
Bin or Binning	A conservative method of calculating population frequency by restricting the database.
Blind Reading of Lanes	Independent readers of autorads, unaware of contents of lanes, render separate opinions which are subsequently compared.
Blind Scoring System	When readers of autorads do not know what is in each lane while visually comparing lanes.
Blot	Same as Southern Blot.
Bluescribe DNA	A type of bacterial DNA.
BSA: Bovine Serum Albumin	A chemical used to stabilize the restriction enzyme and aid in the digestion of DNA.

C

Ceiling Principle	A highly conservative method of calculating population frequencies by substantially restricting the database.
Cellular Debris	Red blood cells, remnants of cell serum, protein and other non-DNA components.

Genetic Fingerprinting:

Chi Square Analysis	Statistical analysis to calculate expected random genetic variations.
Chromosomes	Forty-six structures composed of human DNA.
Cloning	Replication of DNA.
Cocktail Autorad	A single autorad showing two or more loci that have been hybridized at the same time.
Complementary Strand of DNA	Chemically attracted sequence of DNA. e.g. ATTACG which will only combine with TAATGC.
Complete Digestion	The action of a restriction enzyme in completely cutting the DNA at a specific site. See also, Partial Digestion.
Confidence Level	Degree of confidence expressed when two samples of DNA can be said to be the same or different.
Contaminated DNA, Probe, Control or Bacteria	Impure DNA probe, control or bacteria.
Contamination With Plasmid Vector From Insert	Bacterial contamination during production of probes.
Contamination-Cross	Inadvertent mixing of samples; i.e. dirty pipet; lateral movement of DNA across gel.
Control Lane	A known lane. e.g., Male and female DNA run with DYZ1 probe.
Cook's Probe, C-1, or C291	A radioactive probe which mates with DXYS14.
Core Sequence	See One Tandem Repeat.

Cross-Hybridization	A probe which, because of contamination, hybridizes with both human and non-human DNA resulting in strange bands and intensities.
Cumulative Frequency of Occurrence	The sum of the times in which bands have occurred in the population.
Cytosine	One of the four bases found in the DNA helix; will only combine with guanine. See also, adenine, guanine and thymine.

D

D14S1, DXYS14, D2S44, D17S79, DYZ1, or D14S13.	Various loci involved with DNA RFLP forensic identification.
D7S8	A gene located on the seventh chromosome used in PCR and RFLP (AMPFLP)
D1S80	A gene located on the first chromosome used in PCR and RFLP (AMPFLP)
D17Z1	A gene located on the seventeenth chromosome used in PCR and RFLP (AMPFLP)
Database	Information compiled concerning homozygosity, heterozygosity, measurement of fragments of DNA, etc. used for population frequencies and criminal investigations.
Degradation of DNA	The destruction of expected sequences of DNA by an outside source, chemical or otherwise.
Denaturation	The process of unzipping the double helix and exposing a single strand of DNA: accomplished during the Southern Blot procedure.
Detergent	An agent used to cleanse the DNA.

Dextrane Sulfate	Chemical which enhances the probes ability to detect small amounts of DNA on a membrane during hybridization.
Dialysis	The process of separating DNA from cellular debris leaving purified DNA in solution. See Cellular Debris.
Digitizer, Digitizing Mouse, or Tablet.	Device attached to a computer and used to quantify a band on an autorad.
Dirty Autorad	Background marks, contamination, or other items on an autorad other than DNA; also described as "schmutz".
DNA	Deoxyribonucleic acid.
DNA Diagnostics	The use of DNA to diagnose disease.
DNA Fingerprinting, Typing and Forensics	The legal use of DNA testing Identification and as evidence in court.
Dot Blot Assay Membrane	A membrane strip containing known sequences of DNA in dots. See Typing Strip. Used in PCR.
Double Helix	The DNA molecule with two connected complementary strands of DNA.
DQ-Alpha	A gene located in the sixth chromosome used in PCR.
DYZ1	Locus on Y chromosome specific for males.

E

E:	Exposure time of autorad.
ECOR	A restriction enzyme.

Electrophoresis	Electric current applied to agarose gel permitting DNA bands to travel from the negative to positive pole in the gel.
Enzyme	A protein that initiates a chemical reaction.
Enzyme Digestion	The action of the restriction enzyme in cutting the DNA.
Ethidium Bromide	Dye usually used to stain DNA.
Examiner bias	When the examiner of an autorad has an interest in the outcome of a match or non-match.
External Blind Trials	Duplicate samples given to others for duplicate experiments without revealing nature of contents.
Exclusion	The visual and objective measuring of DNA fragments on an autorad which are deemed to be distinguishable, and therefore probably from different people.
Extraction & Isolation of DNA	The process of removing and purifying DNA from the nucleus of a cell.
Extraction Step	That part of the extraction procedure which involves organic chemicals of oil and water solutions, which cause the DNA to stay in the water portion and the cellular debris to be separated into the oil.

F

False Positive, False Exclusion, False Inclusion, False Negative, or False Match.	Erroneous reading of a human or non-human band of DNA on an autorad.
FB	Fresh blood.

Genetic Fingerprinting:

Floating Bins	A conservative method of calculating population frequency.
Fragment	A piece of DNA cut by a restriction enzyme; also-known as a band, or sample.

G

GC (Group Specific Components)	A gene located on the fourth chromosome used in PCR (polymarker).
Gel Fluorescence	Color emitted by DNA in gel after being stained with ethidium bromide stain.
Gender Probes	Probes designed to determine the sex of DNA, be it male or female.
Gene	Section of DNA located within a chromosome which is responsible for some function. e.g., gene for eye color.
Genome	The total pool of genetic information of an organism.
Genotype	Combination of genes found in an individual's DNA concerning specific alleles.
Guanine	One of the four bases found in the DNA helix; will only combine with cytosine. See also, adenine, cytosine, and thymine.
GYPA (Glycophorin A)	A gene located on the fourth chromosome used in PCR (polymarker).

H

HAE-3	A restriction enzyme. See also PST-1.

Hardy-Weinberg Equilibrium	Formula calculating the percentage of alleles in a given population, assumes that population mates freely and randomly and alleles are not linked on same chromosome. Assumes allele frequencies remain constant in a population from generation to generation as long as mating remains random.
HBGG (Hemoglobin G Gamma-globin)	A gene located on the eleventh chromosome used in PCR (polymarker).
Heterozygote	When two alleles in a person are different for one trait, e.g., allele for brown eyes and allele for blue eyes both present.
Heterozygosity	The percentage of the population that is a heterozygote for a particular trait.
Histocompatibility	The compatibility of biological tissue.
Homology	Number of target sites on a fragment of DNA.
Homozygote	When a person receives the same allele from each parent for a particular trait. e.g., two alleles for brown eyes.
Homozygosity	The percentage of the population that is a homozygote for a particular trait.
Human DNA	DNA extracted from a human cell.
Human Gene Mapping Conference	Program to collect data on mapping the human genome.
Hybridization	The process of combining radioactive probes with unzipped strands of DNA to allow for the connection of adenine to thymine and cytosine to guanine.
Hybridized With Homologous Sequence	A probe which attaches to a single strand of DNA with matching base pairs.

Genetic Fingerprinting:

Hypervariable DNA	Same as polymorphism, but refers to a specific site on DNA.

I

Immunogenetics	The relationship between the immune system and genetics.
Inclusion	The visual and objective measurement of DNA fragments on an autorad which are deemed to be indistinguishable and therefore, probably from the same person.
Indistinguishable Bands or Fragments	Bands or fragments of DNA on an autorad that are calculated to be within a scientifically acceptable range to allow a declaration of a match.

K

Karyotype	Analysis of 46 chromosomes in a person.
Kilobase or "Kb" pairs	One thousand base pairs.

L

Laboratory (Lab) Book	Record kept by technicians of experiments performed.
Lambda Hind 3	Marker with known lengths of DNA.
Lane—Loading with DNA	Filling wells on tip of gel with DNA prior to electrophoresis.
Lane of Gel	The path in the gel within which DNA fragments migrate.
Lane Smear	A continuous smear in a lane instead of distinct bands.

Lane to Lane Variation	Uneven running of DNA in lanes during electrophoresis. See band shifting.
Lanes—Coding	Labeling the lanes in the gel.
Lanes—Frowning	Lanes that appear to frown. See band shifting.
Lanes—Smiling	Lanes that appear to smile. See band shifting.
Lanes—Zig-Zag	Lanes that appear to zig-zag. See band shifting.
LDLR (Low Density Lipoprotein Receptor)	A gene located on the nineteenth chromosome used in PCR (polymarker).
Linkage Equilibrium	The transfer of alleles not linked to each other and transferred independently and randomly from parent to child.
Linkage Disequilibrium	The transfer of alleles linked to each other on the same chromosome and not transferred independently and randomly from parent to child.
Loci	Plural of locus.
Locus	A specific site on a chromosome.
Lysing Agent	A chemical used to open the nucleus of the cell and free the DNA.

M

Maniatis, Frisch & Sambrook	Universally recognized published standards for lab protocols.
Manufactured DNA	Synthetically developed sequence of DNA; also known as a synthetic probe or radioactive probe.

Mapping of Human Genome	Effort to determine the function and location of all genes in human DNA.
Marker DNA	A known size of DNA used as a control to determine the size of other fragments or bands of DNA.
Membrane	See nylon filter.
Micro	One one-thousandth.
Mini Satellite Probe	A multi locus probe with multiple band production.
Mitochondrial DNA	A form of DNA found in the nucleus of a cell.
Mixing Experiment, Mix, or Mixed Lane	Mixing known and unknown DNA, loading into one lane, and simultaneously loading known and unknown DNA into separate contiguous lanes to determine if the known and unknown samples co-migrate with the mixed lane.
Mixed Sample	Mixed DNA recovered from two or more people; i.e., semen and vaginal cells; blood from more than one person mixed together at scene.
MLJ Probe	Probe for D14S13 locus.
Molarity	The amount of chemical in one liter of water.
Molecular Biology	The study of living organisms at the molecular level.
Molecular Weight or M.W.	Size of a DNA fragment.
Molecular Weight Markers	See Marker DNA.

Molecular Weight Range	Range of molecular weights of DNA fragments at which a probe is effective.
Molecule	A complex of two or more atoms held together by mutual attraction.
MSP-1	A restriction enzyme.
Mutation	Change in the expected sequence of DNA.

N

Nanogram	One billionth of a gram.
Neurogenetics	Study of relationship between genetics and neurology.
Nitrocellulose Material	The material from which a filter or membrane is composed.
Non-polymorphic Probe	A known base sequence designed to attach to a complementary known base sequence on unzipped DNA, whose function is known and therefore non-polymorphic.
Northern Blot	Same as Southern Blot procedure except deals with RNA instead of DNA.
NRC	National Research Council.
Nucleotide	Combination of A-T or G-C; the steps of the spiral staircase.
Nucleus	The portion of the cell which contains the DNA.
Nucleic Acid Synthesis	Method of cloning DNA.
Nylon Filter	The filter to which the DNA is transferred during the Southern Blotting procedure. Also known as a filter or membrane.

O

Oligo	Designation for a synthetic probe.
O.D.	Optical density.
O/N	Overnight exposure of autorad.
Opacity	The quality of transmitting diffused light.
One Tandem Repeat or One Repeat Unit	A single sequence of base pairs that repeat themselves.

P

Partial Digestion	An undesirable result obtained when the restriction enzyme fails to cut the DNA at a specific site.
PCR	Polymerase Chain Reaction; method of cloning small amounts of DNA to produce large amounts of the same DNA.
Peer Review	System of review of articles submitted for publication in a scientific journal.
Phage Lambda DNA	Bacterial DNA used for marker lanes.
Phenotype	Gene which expresses a dominant trait.
Phosphate & Deoxyribose Sugar	Balustrade or handrails of the DNA ladder.
PIC	Polymorphism Information Content.
Plasmid	An entity present in bacteria.
Polymarker	Multiple genes examined in PCR.
Polymer	A chain of hydrocarbons which form the backbone of the DNA helix.

Polymerase Chain Reaction	See PCR.
Polymorphic Probe	A known base sequence designed to attach to a complementary base sequence on an unknown fragment of unzipped DNA.
Polymorphism	A section of the DNA that varies greatly from person to person.
Population Genetics	The study of the frequency of genes and alleles in various populations.
Pores in Gel	Tiny comb-like holes in an agarose gel designed to slow the movement of DNA fragments during electrophoresis.
Post Mortem Blood Sample	Sample of blood removed from a deceased during autopsy.
Pre-hybridization Solution	A solution added to a membrane to aid in hybridization.
Primer	Sequence specific probe in PCR which recognizes known section of gene.
Probe	Sequence specific DNA which attaches to unzipped DNA.
Product Breakdown	DNA deterioration which causes extra bands.
Product Rule	A liberal method of calculating population frequency.
Proficiency Testing	Tests to aid in assuring competence of technicians performing experiments.
Proteinase	An enzyme which digests protein.
Protocols	Procedures to be followed by technicians when performing experiments.

Genetic Fingerprinting:

PST-1	A restriction enzyme designed to cut the DNA at a specific site See also HAE 3.
Purified Probe	Synthetic or manufactured probe.
Purines	The chemicals Adenine (A) and Guanine (G).
Pyrimidines	The chemicals Thymine (T) and (Cytosine (C).

Q

Quality Controls or Quality Assurance	Controls and checks which aid in assuring the reliability of the experimental process.
Quantitatively Confirm Visual Match	Confirming a visual match by computer analysis.

R

Radioactive DNA	DNA which has hybridized with a radioactive probe.
rDNA	Ribosomal DNA.
RDNA	Recombinant DNA or DNA which is spliced from different organisms.
Reader Bias	See Examiner bias.
Recombinant DNA	DNA that is spliced with other DNA.
Restriction Enzyme	An enzyme that cuts the DNA at a specific, known, sequence site.
Re-hybridized	Washing a membrane of one radioactive probe and repeating the process of hybridization with another probe on the same membrane.

RFLP	Restriction Fragment Length Polymorphism.
Ph System; Positive or Negative	An antigen that may or may not be present in blood plasma and is readily determined.
RNA	Ribonucleic acid
Rocker	A machine which rocks the membrane after hybridization to insure full coverage of the membrane.

S

Satellite DNA	DNA fragments of lengths similar to those being probed for, which appear as extra bands on an autorad.
Sequence of Base Pairs	The sequence of A, T, G, and C in the DNA molecule.
Sequence Specific	Probe with a sequence exactly Oligonucleotide (SSO) matching the sequence of the target DNA.
Serial Dilution	Diluting a solution of DNA to reduce intensity or size of band, to allow a more accurate comparison of degraded DNA.
Signal	Radioactive emission indicating tagged probe attached to DNA fragment.
Single Strand of DNA	One strand of DNA from the double stranded helix of DNA.
Sizing	Measuring size of band.
Slant of Migration	See Band shifting.
Sodium Perchlorate	A preservative added to DNA following dialysis to permit storage of DNA; anti-bacterial agent.

Genetic Fingerprinting:

Solo Probe	A single probe, not a cocktail.
Southern Blot	The process of transferring the DNA fragments from the agarose gel to a membrane or cellulose filter, leaving the fragments in the exact position of their gel migration.
Spectrophotometer	A device used to determine the quantity of DNA in a solution.
Spike	Deliberate adding of sample to an unknown, as a control.
Split Samples	Separating samples of DNA between technicians to allow for independent testing of unknown samples.
Standard Deviation	Statistical devices used to determine precision of test; the smaller the standard deviation, the greater the precision. Note: Precision is not the same as accuracy.
Star Activity	Imprecise cutting of DNA; failure of restriction enzyme to cut at usual site causing unexpected additional bands.
Stripping Membrane	See Washing membrane.
Sub-Population	A smaller segment of a related population (Hispanics from Spain versus Hispanics from Ecuador).
Synthetic Probe	See manufactured DNA.

T

TAQ Polymerase	An enzyme used in PCR to permit base pairs to find complementary sequences extending target DNA.

Thermocycler	Machine that heats & cools DNA to permit hybridization in PCR.
Thymine	One of the bases present in DNA; will only combine with adenine. See also, cytosine, guanine, adenine.
Transfection	DNA strain grown within Escherichea coli (E. coli), a bacterium.
TWGDAM	Technical Working Group on DNA Analysis and Methods.
Typing Strip	A membrane containing dots of known sequences of DNA. Used in PCR. See also Dot Blot Strip.

U

Unzipped Strands of DNA	Single strands of DNA which have been chemically separated from the double helix.

V

Vector	Circular piece of DNA that has a plasmid that is used for the replication of DNA inside a bacterium.
Visual Match	Visual analysis of autorad to determine if DNA bands have co-migrated in lanes.
VNTR	Variable Number of Tandem Repeats: repeat sequences in the DNA occurring at random.

W

Wahlund's Theory for Population Frequencies	A formula designed to determine if there is a deviation from Hardy-Weinberg Equilibrium.

Washing   See Washing Membrane.

Washing Membrane   A solution which removes radioactive probes from a membrane without disturbing the position of the DNA fragments. See Re-hybridized membrane.

X & Y

X and Y Chromosomes   The chromosomes which determine the sex of an individual.

Yield Gel   An agarose gel used to determine the quantity and quality of DNA.

1. California, Colorado, Florida, Georgia, Hawaii, Illinois, Indiana, Iowa, Kansas, Maryland, Massachusetts, Michigan, Minnesota, Missouri, Montana, Oregon, New Hampshire, New Jersey (PCR), New Mexico, New York, North Carolina, Ohio, Pennsylvania, South Carolina, South Dakota, Texas (RFLP and PCR), Virginia (RFLP and PCR), Washington, West Virginia, and Wyoming.

2. Arizona (as to Cellmark), Colorado, Iowa, Michigan, Missouri, New York, Ohio, South Carolina, Texas, and West Virginia.

3. Colorado, Hawaii, Illinois, Indiana, Iowa, Ohio, Minnesota, Missouri, New Hampshire, New York, Oregon, Pennsylvania, South Carolina, Washington, West Virginia, and Wyoming.

4. Alabama, Minnesota, New Mexico (as to the FBI), North Carolina, South Carolina, South Dakota, and West Virginia.

5. Arkansas, Arizona, Delaware, The District of Columbia, Nebraska, New Hampshire, and Pennsylvania.

6. *California v. Soto*, 30 Cal. App. 4th 340, 35 Cal.Rptr.2d. 846 (1994), petition for review granted, 890 P.2d 1115 (3/16/95); *California v. Wilds*, 37 Cal.Rptr.2d. 351 (Cal. App. 2 Dist. 1995); *California v. Marlow*, 1995 WL 238692, (Cal.App. 6th Dist. 1995); *California v. Amundson, infra; California v. Burks*, 1995 WL 464138 (Cal. App. 4th Dist. 1995).

7. I have included the scientific language used to express the most important features of the DNA analysis process in foot notes. In order to understand this material, you have to come to grips with the scientific language.

8. Identified chemically as deoxycytosine triphosphate, deoxyguanosine triphosphate, deoxyadenosine triphosphate, and deoxythymidine triphosphate. In scientific nation they are written as dCTP, dGTP, dATP, and dTTP. The "d" means "deoxyribose" rather than "ribose" sugar.

9. Yet the difference in the genetic spelling of the genome between a human and a chimpanzee is about one percent; the difference between a human and a mouse is about two percent; the difference

in the genetic spelling between one human and another is a tiny fraction of one percent; and humans contain some of the genetic spelling for ants, fish, and plants. This tends to support the observation that we all came from a common source.

10. The chromosomes are divided into two general groups: the non-sex typing chromosomes are called "autosomes." Somatic, or non-reproductive, human cells contain 22 pairs of autosomes and one pair of sex chromosomes. The total number of paired chromosomes in these cells is called "diploid". The reproductive cells, the sperm and the egg, are called "gametes" or "germ cells" and contain the "haploid" chromosome number; in other words they contain one copy of each autosome and one sex typing chromosome. If the sperm cell containing the "Y" chromosome joins with the egg, the offspring is male. If the sperm cell containing the "X" chromosome joins with the egg, the offspring is female.

11. The chromosomes themselves vary from 50 million to 300 million base pairs in size. They are numbered according to size.

12. Identical twins are the exception to this statement. Since they are both the product of single union between one egg and one sperm cell, the twins' DNA is identical.

13. The epithelium is tissue that forms the surface of an organ or organism. Here it is the vagina. Epithelial cells occur throughout the body, for example on the outer skin or the cells lining the gut and respiratory cavities.

14. PCR refers to the Polymerase Chain Reaction, the other major method for analysis of forensic DNA samples. The discussion of PCR begins at Section 4.

15. A more extensive discussion of band shifting begins at Section 6.

16. As of 1995, the following loci were most frequently examined in forensic laboratories in the United States: D2S44, D14S13, D10S28, D17S79, D1S7, D4S139, D18S27 and D5S110, DXYS14 and DYZ1. Other loci include D4S163 and D10S7.

17. Jeffreys, *Individual Specific Fingerprints of Human DNA*, 36 Nature 76-

79 (July 4, 1975) and Jeffreys, Turner, and Debenham, *The Efficiency of Multilocus DNA Fingerprint Probes for Individualization and Establishment of Family Relationships, Determined from Extensive Casework*, 48 Am. J. Hum. Genet. 824 (1991) contain a discussion of the multi-locus probes.

18. In the language of science, this molecule is a heterodimer (a protein made up of paired polypeptides [a polymer made of amino acids linked together by peptide bonds] that differ in their amino acid sequences) composed of one alpha chain and one beta chain. It is expressed in B-lymphocytes (cells that produce antibodies), macrophages (large leukocytes [white blood cells] found throughout the body that process the antigens that produce the immune response), thymic epithelium (the outer surface of the thymus gland) and activated T-cells (the part of the immunity system that rejects grafts and organ transplants). It serves as an integral membrane protein for binding as well as presenting antigen peptide fragments to the T-cell receptor of CD4 T lymphocytes. At the DNA level most of the polymorphism of the HLA DQ Alpha locus is localized on the second exon (the portion of a split gene that passes in the messenger RNA and becomes part of the structural RNA; the second exon contains the information that is translated into the amino acid sequence of a protein) encoding the NH2 terminal outer domain.

19. These include D1S80, D7S8, D17Z1, the Low Density Lipoprotein Receptor (LDLR), Glycophorin A (GYPA), Hemoglobin G Gammaglobin (HBGG), Group Scientific Component (GC), and the short tandem repeats (STRs) found in the Apolipoprotein B (APO-B) and (HUM THOI) loci.

20. Specifically this kit detects six of the ten known alleles that make up the DQ Alpha locus that codes for the alpha chain of the DQ Alpha heterodimer protein that is one of the Class II antigens that constitute the major histocompatibility locus on the sixth chromosome. These are discussed in detail in the text.

21. This kit detects the alleles of D7S8, Glycophorin A (GYPA) (190 base pairs) and Group Specific Globulin (GC) (138 base pairs)—both found on chromosome 4, Low Density Lipoprotein Receptor (LDLR) (214 base pairs)—found on chromosome 19, and Hemoglobin G-gamma Globulin (HBGG) (172 base pairs)—found on chromosome

11. The materials in the kit must be stored at 2 degrees C to 8 degrees C—a line of questioning that may come up on cross-examination.

22. The Quantiblot kit, produced by Perkin Elmer, is used to determine how much DNA is available for analysis. This kit analyzes D17Z1. The probe contains the following genetic code: 5'-TAGAAG-CATTCTCAGAAACTACTTTCT GATGATTGCATTC-3'.

23. The most recent nomenclature system adopted in 1990 by the World Health Organization HLA Nomenclature Committee now designates the DQ alpha locus as "DQA1" and the previously known DXa locus as "DQA2." The alleles are now designated as DQA1*0101 (previously A1.1); *0102 (previously A1.2); *0103 (previously A1.3); DQA1*0201 (previously A.2); *0301 (previously A.3); DQA1*0401 (previously A.4.2); DQQA1*0501 (previously A.4.1); and DqA1*0601 (previously A.4.3). The expert may be more comfortable with the new terminology. Used herein is the DQ Alpha label and the old allele labels because most of the scientific literature that is likely to be relevant in trials conducted in 1994-95 refer to the locus by the old designation.

24. DNA is a one-way molecule that has two ends: one known as 3' and one known as 5'. The prime marking means that the measurement is taken from the sugar molecule rather than the nucleotide.

25. Oligonucleotides are sequences of up to twenty nucleotides joined by phosphodiester bonds (i.e., a chemical linkage of known structure that forms a covalent bond with the sugars in the DNA molecule).

26. The ones used in PCR replication are dADP, dCTP, dGTP and dTTP.

27. *Thermus aquaticus* lives in the hot springs in Yellowstone National Park. As a result, it does not break down when exposed to high heat and may be used during the replication sequence. The Klenow fragment of E. Coli, the original polymerase used in the extension process, was thermolabile (destroyed when heated above 55 degrees C); thus the use of this polymerase required more careful control and more repetitions of the process to achieve the desired quantity of amplified DNA. The discovery of Taq has largely eliminated these problems.

Genetic Fingerprinting:

28. The template-directed manner refers to the macromolecular structure that allows DNA and RNA to communicate to create a new double strand of DNA; thus the natural growth process is duplicated by the PCR process. The process has been described (in 263 *Science* 1565 [1994]) as "a technique for taking over nature's machine for replicating genetic material and shifting it into overdrive." This down-to-earth description of the process should help the jury understand its fundamental nature.

29. Why do they make so much? Because the PCR process can only be done one time on a sample. Restarting the process once it has stopped requires a new sample to start on, and in forensic cases there is none. If more than 10 billion copies of forensic DNA is needed, the process must be continued for more cycles until enough DNA is obtained.

30. The Southern Blot process may be used to analyze PCR amplified DNA. Current test kits are designed not to use this process, however. One problem with the use of Southern Blotting to analyze DQ Alpha, is that the restriction enzyme HAE III, used by the FBI, does not recognize any site for the DQ Alpha 3 allele.

31. The blue color for the dot is created by the introduction of a streptavidin-horseradish peroxidase. This stuff comes from the same plant that we eat as horseradish, a point that can be made so the jury will feel more at home with the scientific language. The system operates by adding biotin which binds to the 5' end of the DNA molecule. Biotin has an extremely strong affinity and is highly specific for streptavid which is attached to the horseradish.

32. The March 18, 1994 issue of *Science* (Vol. 263 at p. 1564) reports that Dr. Wayne Barnes, of the Washington University School of Medicine in St. Louis, Mo., has successfully replicated stretches of DNA weighing 35 KB by PCR by using a mixture of the polymerases Klentaq 1 and *Pfu*. Roche Molecular Systems and Perkin-Elmer, the producers of two of the commonly used PCR kits are experimenting with his ideas. If this research is reliably reproducible in the forensic setting, scientists should be able to amplify small quantities of DNA containing sufficient weight to allow for RFLP analysis.

33. A nanogram is one billionth of a gram. The protocols for the

Quantiblot Kit assert that it can amplify samples containing 0.15 to 10.0 nanograms of human DNA.

34. The Qauntibot kit can also be used to perform this function.

35. Reynolds, Sensabaugh, and Blake. *Analysis of Genetic Markers in Forensic DNA Samples Using the Polymerase Chain Reaction*, 63 Analytical Chemistry No. 1. (Jan. 1, 1991).

36. According to the protocols for the Amplitype PM kit, PCR amplified DNA may be stored for two weeks at 2 degrees to 8 degrees C or for six months at -20 degrees C.

37. To guard against contamination due to laboratory error, the April, 1992 Report of the National Academy of Science recommends having PCR analysis done independently in two separate laboratories each starting with a piece of the unprocessed evidence sample. "Given the inexpensiveness of typing, serious consideration should be given to independent replication of results—at least during the early stages of this technology."

38. As the areas of the genome available for PCR analysis increase, this problem will lessen. For example, in 1994, CBR Laboratories in Boston used PCR to examine the following markers in addition to DQ Alpha: LDLR, GYPA, HBGG, D7S8, and GC. From these eleven alleles they calculated that the genetic enscription at issue would be present in 1 out of 906,000 Caucasians, 1 out of 11,810 African Americans, and 1 out of 630,700 Hispanics.

39. This type of error can be eliminated, by performing the extraction, amplification and typing steps in separate rooms or biological hoods which prohibit foreign substances from entering the area where the process is performed. Separate sets of pipettors should be used for extraction, reaction preparation and for handling the amplified DNA in another room. If the lab does not take these steps at a minimum, expect significant controversy. If the defense wants to test the DNA in a lab that does not employ these safeguards, there is a basis for the court to refuse the request and directing that the defense tests be performed in a lab that meets these criteria.

40. One solution that can be considered in rape cases (with the victim's

consent, of course,) is to take multiple vaginal swabs and to hold some of them in reserve in COLD AND DRY conditions as possible replacements.

41. As of 1994, the FBI was reporting an exclusion rate of 33%. Expect this fact to be aired on cross-examination.

42. Reynolds, Sensabaugh, and Blake, *supra*, Fn. 35. Conversely, in the November 1991 edition of the *Journal of Forensic Sciences*, Catherine Comey and Bruce Budlowle of the FBI caution that when the mixed samples are both homozygous for an allele or when a homozygous sample shares its allele with a heterozygous sample, the mix cannot be detected, the possibility of a mixed sample must be considered if only one genetic locus is typed. See *infra* Fn. 44.

43. Heme refers to iron containing porphyrin molecules that form the oxygen binding portion of hemoglobin.

44. Comey and Budlowle, *Validation Studies on the Analysis of the HLA DQ Alpha Locus Using the Polymerase Chain Reaction*, 36 Journal of Forensic Sciences pp. 1644, 1647 (Nov. 1991).

45. For example, the protocols for the Amplitype kit require allowing the machine to warm up for 99 minutes and 59 seconds. No more, no less. The timing should be controlled by a computer chip in the machine that tells it when to do what. CBR Labs in Boston also has a running graph printed that demonstrates that the timing of the process was correct. The graph looks like the results generated by a polygraph or lie detector.

46. This statement is not as confusing as it appears upon a first reading. Remember that DNA is a one-way molecule running from 3' to 5' and that each strand of the DNA double helix runs in opposite directions. Thus when the Taq runs from 3' to 5' during the amplification process, it is running in opposite directions on each strand. You can think of this as running forward on one strand and backwards on the other. When it reaches a damaged site through which it cannot extend or the end of a fragment that is unnaturally short due to degradation, it has to stop too soon. On the next cycle the process is repeated using the incompletely extended first fragments as the new template, and the Taq will again run to the artificial stopping point.

This process continues until a full length product is produced. This product is full of holes, however. To use the alphabet as a paradigm, the full 26 letter amplified DNA might look like ABC-HIJ-LMN-TUV-ABC-LIM-TUV-ABC etc. In other words, some of the As, Ts, Cs, and Gs that should be there have been omitted.

47. Remember the nature of the hydrogen bond causes purines to bind to purines (three bonds) and pyrimidines to bind to pyrimidines (two bonds). If our bacterium has happened to eat one of these bonds, the chemical magnetism is altered. The scientists will tell you that this cannot happen because the hydrogen bond created by the mismatch of a purine to a pyrimidine is too weak to withstand the heat generated by the PCR process; nonetheless allele drop out remains an area of concern if the mixture is not heated to the specified temperature of 94 degrees C. Tests have demonstrated that, at temperatures of 88 degrees C. or below, neither the 1.1 or the 4 allele was amplified; at 88 degrees C., however, there was preferential amplification of the 4 allele as compared with the 1.1 allele. Be prepared to hear cross-examination on this point.

48. Two common problems that can occur at this stage of the process are incomplete digestion and star activity. The TWGDAM guidelines do not mention them as such, but since they can be a subject for cross-examination, they deserve brief mention. Incomplete digestion occurs when the enzyme does not cut the DNA in every place that it should, and thus is "incomplete". Star activity occurs when, under some conditions, the enzyme cuts the DNA at anomalous recognition sites, i.e., in the "wrong" place. HAE III has been criticized for causing star activity. The effect of both problems is to cut fragments that are not the proper size, and hence which do not migrate to their proper places on the gel. The result is the bands appear at the wrong place and can lead to false inclusion or exclusion. See "Partial Digestion". See the New York case, *People v. Watson, supra*

49. Though not a part of the TWGDAM guidelines, in sex cases and in cases where males and females are victims or suspects, the human DNA should be both male and female. This allows for fixing the location of the XX and XY chromosomes and authoritatively demonstrates which forensic sample comes from the male and which comes from the female. (See *People v. Castro, supra*)

Genetic Fingerprinting:

50. The risk of a genuine false identification through band shift is actually infinitesimal. The typical RFLP court room match is made by comparing bands which are created by different probes over at least three different gels and which appear at various places over the entire length of each gel. For band shift to result in a false identification, the phenomenon would have to repeat itself in consistent fashion over the entire length of a number of gels. Further, the forensic DNA and the suspect DNA would have to vary constantly with respect to each other over the entire length of more than one gel. Theoretically this is possible, but it is more theoretical than real. To date, no case has uncovered such a scenario.

51. A standard deviation is defined by ASCLD's glossary as the square root of the average squared difference between the individual observations and the population mean (i.e., take each variation, square it, average the squares, and take the square root of that). Three standard deviations is the scientific norm for this procedure, however.

52. A thorough discussion of a "bin" begins at G§ 7(c).

53. Note that each probe examines a different chromosome in order to avoid linkage disequilibrium.

54. To understand why this is so, assume that DNA is a cloth tape measure that stretches for thirty-six inches. The FBI's enzyme may be said to cut it in three inch increments while Lifecodes' enzyme cuts it in six inch increments. Thus Lifecodes' enzyme will reveal matches at inches four, five and six as well as the matches at inches one, two, and three that are revealed under both FBI and Lifecodes technology.

55. See, e.g.: *U.S. v. Porter*, 618 A.2d 629 (D.C. Ct. Ap. 12/22/92) (FBI pop/gen estimate of 1 in 30 million is unreliable in view of product rule controversy as reflected in *Lewontin/Hartl* (*Science* 12/20/91). However, court concludes that a more conservative estimate would be admissible, and remands for further hearings on this matter. *California v. Barney*, 8 Cal. App.4th 798 (Ct. App. 1st Dist. 1992), (both Cellmark and FBI tests inadmissible due to use of the product rule and lack of scientific agreement supporting it. *California v. Pizarro*, 10 Cal.App.4th 57, 12 Cal.Rptr.2d 436 (Ct. App.5th Dist.1992)(rejects FBI test and pop/gen database for Blacks when defendant is a member

of a sub-group (Blacks or Nigerian descent). "It is evident that there is no generally accepted scientific theory on population genetics involving broad racial and ethnic groups as opposed to the argument of structure. We cannot resolve on this record the question of general acceptance in the scientific community. We conclude on the present record that the admission of the RFLP test results together with the statistical conclusions drawn therefrom was error." *Massachusetts v. Lanigan*, 413 Mass. 154, 596 N.E.2d 311 (Sup. Ct. 1992) (using a *Frye* standard, refuses to admit FBI test and evidence of match because of the scientific controversy over population substructure on the Hardy-Weinberg equilibrium of a Caucasian database. This issue has been resolved by the same court after a remand hearing (419 Mass. 15, 641 N.E.2d 1342 (1994)).

56. Much of the controversy that surrounds the substructure controversy may have been laid to rest as the result of joint article published in *Nature* by Dr. Eric Lander, of Whitehead Institute in Cambridge (a prominent early critic of the then prevailing methods to calculate the population genetics) and Dr. Bruce Budowle, the chief of the FBI lab. The two former adversaries have agreed that the scientific controversies that surrounded the early attempts at population genetics analysis have been resolved. While they agree that the ceiling principle should be used, they also agree that an expert should also be allowed to testify about calculations derived from the product rule. Lander and Budowle, *DNA Fingerprinting Dispute Laid to Rest*, 371 *Nature* 735 (October 27, 1994). This article presents many fruitful areas which may be used in direct and cross-examination of the experts.

57. Cellmark may have employed a similar methodology, pursuant to the case law.

58. No pre-trial DNA hearing was conducted.

59. In *People v. Mohit, infra* SectionJ § 29(a), the court noted: "Does it matter in a criminal case if a jury is told 1 in 67 million or 1 in 100,000? In most cases, probably not."

60. This case is also noteworthy because the complainant suffered from night blindness and was unable to see her rapist. She described the rapist as young, without facial hair, 5'8" tall, weighing 150 pounds,

with a Spanish accent, and small, soft, delicate hands. In fact, the defendant was 30 years old, weighed 210 pounds, was 5'10" tall, and had a mustache. Also the defendant worked as a garbage collector, which caused his hands to be rough and calloused. See also *Toranzo v. Florida*, 608 So.2d 83 (Fla. Ct. App. 1992).

61. For an analysis of this issue, see Sheindlin, *DNA Forensic Evidence: Are Statistics Really Necessary?*, N.Y.L.J.,8/4/95, Pg. 1, Col. 1.

62. See, *Massachusetts v. Drayton, infra*; Sheindlin, *DNA Forensic Evidence: Are Statistics Necessary? Supra*, J § 12.

63. The ceiling method for population genetics calculation was recommended by the April, 1992 report of the National Academy of Sciences Committee entitled *DNA Technology in Forensic Science* as a practical and sound approach for accounting for error based on possible population substructure. It proceeds upon the assumption that the multiplication rule will yield conservative (i.e., pro-defendant) estimates, even for a substructure population, provided that the allele frequencies used in the multiplication calculation exceed the allele frequencies in any of the population subgroups.

    The report advocates taking random samples from 100 persons in each of 15-20 targeted subpopulations which are relatively homogenous genetically, and taking the largest frequency. The report uses the following illustration:

    "Suppose that two loci have been studied in three population sample with the following results:

	Population 1	**Population 2**	**Population 3**
Locus 1			
Allele a	1%	5%	11%
Allele b	5%	8%	10%
Locus 2			
Allele c	3%	4%	4%
Allele d	2%	15%	7%

    For the genotype consisting of a/b at locus 2, the ceiling principle would assign ceiling values of 11% for allele a, 10% for allele b, 5%

for allele c, and 15% for allele d and would apply the multiplication rule to yield a genotype frequency of $[2(0.11)(0.10)][2(0.5)(0.15)]=0.00033$, or about 1 in 3,000. Note that the frequency used for allele c is 5% rather than 4%, to reflect the recommended lower bound for each allele frequency."

Any lack of discriminating power caused by this very conservative approach to the multiplication rule can be remedied by employing additional probes.

64. In *People v. Gino Greco*, ___ Misc.2d ___ (Erie Co. Ct. Ind. No. 90-0122-001, Decided November 4, 1992) (N.O.R.) in the course of holding that probable cause existed to seize defendant's blood, the court ruled that DNA identification evidence would be admissible unless excluded for some other reason. See also *People v. Ehrenberg*, N.Y.L.J. 12/3/93, p.30, col.3.

65. After pleading guilty, the defendant admitted that the blood on his watch was in fact the decedent's blood. Thus, in this case, the DNA test resulted in a false exclusion as the disputed bands were not human bands as claimed by the experts. In both *Castro* and *Wesley*, the DNA evidence was merely corroborative of the defendant's guilt. In *Wesley*, the conviction was affirmed because the DNA evidence was merely supportive of otherwise overwhelming evidence of guilt.

66. Since the defendant was convicted without the use of the DNA evidence, the court's ruling will not be reviewed by an appellate court.

67. It is interesting to note that in *Wesley*, the statistical numbers were reduced by a factor of ten but the "ceiling principle" recommended by the NRC was not used.

68. For a further analysis of these issues see, Sheindlin, *Comparing Castro and Wesley: Is There Really a Conflict?* N.Y.L.J., March 27, 1995, Pg. 1, Col. 1.

69. For a discussion of the disagreement amongst scientists about whether use of the Hardy Weinberg equation and the product rule may be validly applied to this evidence in a forensic setting see G7(a) *supra*. Compare, Lewontin and Hartl: *Population Genetics in Forensic DNA Typing*, 254*Science* 1745 (12/20/91), with Chakraborty and

Kidd: *The Utility of DNA Typing in Forensic Work*, 254 *Science* 1735 12/20/91). But see, Lander and Budowle, *DNA Fingerprinting Dispute Laid to Rest*, 371 *Nature* 753 (10/27/94).

70. On August 12, 1993, the Supreme Court of Washington upheld the constitutionality of Wash. Rev. Code Ann. 43.43. 754, which authorizes the state to extract blood from convicted sex offenders for the creation of a DNA databank. *Washington v. Olivas*, 122 Wash. 73, 856 P.2d 1076 (1993).

71. The trial court had refused to admit the FBI's conclusion that there was a 1 in 2600 probability that the semen in the victim's panties came from someone other that the defendant, but allowed testimony concerning the "match." This caused the government to argue on summation that the defendant "fits the profile of the DNA." The court refused to review defendant's claims regarding the admission of the match without the statistical evidence, finding that the doctrine of invited error precluded its review.

72. The Supreme Court remanded the case for application of the *Daubert* standards. Upon remand, the U.S. Court of Appeals ruled that the plaintiffs failed to establish that their expert's opinion was scientifically reliable and granted summary judgment to defendant. *Daubert v. Merrill Dow*, 43 F.3d 1311 (9th Cir 1995).